Job-Hunting for the
So-Called Handicapped

OTHER BOOKS BY RICHARD NELSON BOLLES

What Color Is Your Parachute? A Practical Manual for Job-Hunters and Career-Changers

The What Color Is Your Parachute? Workbook

Job-Hunting on the Internet

The Career Counselor's Handbook
(with Howard Figler)

*The Three Boxes of Life,
and How to Get Out of Them*

How to Find Your Mission in Life

OTHER BOOKS BY DALE S. BROWN

Learning a Living: A Guide to Planning Your Career and Finding a Job for People with Learning Disabilities, Attention Deficit Disorder, and Dyslexia

Learning Disabilities and Employment

I Know I Can Climb the Mountain

Steps to Independence for People with Learning Disabilities

Job-Hunting for the
So-Called Handicapped

OR PEOPLE WHO HAVE DISABILITIES

2nd edition

Richard Nelson Bolles & Dale S. Brown

TEN SPEED PRESS
Berkeley   Toronto

Ten Speed Press
P.O. Box 7123
Berkeley, California 94707
www.tenspeed.com

Distributed in Australia by Simon and Schuster Australia, in Canada by Ten Speed Press Canada, in New Zealand by Southern Publishers Group, in South Africa by Real Books, in Southeast Asia by Berkeley Books, and in the United Kingdom and Europe by Airlift Book Company.

Typesetting by Star Type, Berkeley
Cover design by Thomjon Borges
Printed in Canada

Library of Congress Cataloging-in-Publication Data

Bolles, Richard Nelson.
    Job-hunting for the so-called handicapped / Richard Nelson Bolles,
Dale Susan Brown. -- Rev. ed.
            p. cm.
Includes index.
    ISBN 1-58008-195-9 (alk. paper)
    1. Vocational guidance for the handicapped -- United States.
2. Handicapped -- Employment -- United States. 3. Job hunting -- United States.
I. Brown, Dale S. II. Title.
    HV1568.5 .B65 2001
    650.14'087 -- dc21
    2001002799

First printing this edition, 2001

1 2 3 4 5 6 7 8 9 10 -- 05 04 03 02 01

Contents

Acknowledgments

We would like to acknowledge the staff at Ten Speed Press. Without their hard work, this book would not be possible. We would like to thank Aaron Wehner, whose editing and restructuring was very helpful. The folks at Ten Speed are a major reason this book is in your hands today.

Dick would like to acknowledge all of those with so-called handicaps who, when this book was first proposed some years ago, sat down with him in a series of group meetings, and told him what works and what doesn't work. Without their input, this book would never have been created in the first place.

Dale would like to acknowledge her family of origin, her parents Joy Gilman and Bertram S. Brown, M.D,. and her sisters, Laurie Browngoehl, Wendy Brown-Blau, and Tracy Brown. Barbara Schrader provided counsel and guidance during the writing process. And, she is also grateful to the members of her network within the disability community. She wishes she could name them all, but that would be impossible.

RICHARD NELSON BOLLES
DALE S. BROWN

A Word About This Edition

A FOREWORD BY DALE S. BROWN

My acquaintance with Richard Bolles, the coauthor of this book, began during my second search for full-time employment in 1980. My work as a volunteer had given me a new career goal -- becoming an advocate for people with disabilities.

I had founded the Association of Learning Disabled Adults (ALDA), one of the first self-help groups for people with learning disabilities. I was **passionate** about helping people with learning disabilities. While publicizing my group, I had discovered that being a person who overcame severe learning disabilities was a point of pride, not a flaw to hide. Sharing my experience inspired individuals and pushed policy makers to think more deeply about laws and regulations. I was **determined** to find a full-time job in the field of "disability" in order to work on my mission -- **proving** people did not outgrow learning disabilities and **improving** the lives of adults who had learning disabilities.

But how? My first job-hunt after college graduation used traditional techniques -- answering classified advertisements, mailing resumes, visiting people and asking them if they knew of openings, and following up with every lead in a disciplined manner. Interestingly enough, the job came to me through an organization that rejected me! The woman who interviewed me told my future boss, Diane, about me. She said our personalities would match. Diane called me up. We got together and she hired me for a federal contract that lasted three years.

A year before the contract ended, however, the prospect of searching for new work made me nervous. On the one hand, I was in the enviable position of looking for work while holding a job. I didn't have to face the stigma of being unemployed. On the other hand, I **had** to find a job before my contract ended -- unless, of course, a way of wage-free living could be figured out!

Founding ALDA and attracting people to it had involved extensive public relations. The small local group became a model for others, and we formed a larger organization -- the National Network of Learning Disabled Adults (NNLDA). My face had been on TV and in newspapers as a person with learning disabilities who was leading a self-help group. This put me in a similar position to people with more obvious disabilities. As a matter of integrity, it seemed necessary to disclose my learning disabilities. Otherwise my future bosses might have found out by hearing me on a radio show!

Luckily, while browsing in a bookstore, I found *What Color Is Your Parachute?* I read the book and decided immediately to follow its directions. I followed them precisely, much as a cook follows a recipe. After a thorough assessment of my strengths and weaknesses, and deciding where I wanted to work, I chose my job objective. It was to become a full-time writer in a national organization that specialized in people, preferably adults, with disabilities in the Washington, DC, area. Fortunately that is where most of the national organizations are.

While reading the book, I felt Bolles's presence. It was as if he were speaking to me as my friend and mentor.

My initial research on employers that might hire me was discouraging. Twenty years ago little staff, money, or attention was focused on the issue of disability. Almost no organizations hired full-time writers. Most organizations were small. They contracted their writing out.

However, locating them by interviewing for information (as Bolles advised), was perfect for me. I was able to discuss my learning disabilities and my experience founding ALDA in context. Some people gave me negative responses, such as, "How can you be learning disabled--you graduated from college?" After explaining to them that people with learning disabilities were intelligent, I handled any other prejudiced or ignorant statements they made. Even if they still held to their beliefs, they would often refer me to people who they thought could help me. And of course, nobody referred me to employers who wouldn't like me--or who would discriminate against me.

Most people ignored my learning disabilities and paid attention to my success founding a national organization. They were flattered because my research allowed me to specifically and sincerely praise their most beloved and important work. My questions made them think about topics of interest to them. It helped that I was enthusiastic, willing to learn, cheerful, and honored to meet them. I sent **everyone**, even those who gave me minimal help, a detailed thank-you note. As the process continued, each interview gave me lots of new information. So, some people, interviewed later in the process, asked me questions and benefited from our encounter.

I found one government agency that hired writers--the President's Committee on Employment of the Handicapped. Before starting to talk to their employees, I visited their publication room and picked up all of their literature. Subsequently

I read a stack of their materials, which was, literally, two feet tall. Bob Ruffner's name came up occasionally. He was the director of their communications department--and clearly the person who had the power to hire me.

So I wrote him a letter including quotes from some things he wrote that impressed me along with a description of why I liked what he wrote and his philosophy. My letter requested a meeting. He called me and we met. I then interviewed almost everyone in the agency for information--and kept writing him letters with ideas on what I would do, if he hired me.

Several months later, he told me about a vacancy. I did have to fill out an application and compete for it, but several months later, he offered me a position--one that paid about 30 percent more than I was making.

This creative approach that Bolles proposed was not only helpful to me in finding my job. It taught me a process that I've used over and over again throughout my life since that day. On my first day at work, I already had friends and a full Rolodex of contacts. When I received assignments, even when they were in fields where I knew nothing, the skills my job-hunting had taught me made the research and writing easy.

I became a missionary--as zealous about **interviewing for information** as about learning disabilities. Every time someone asked me about how I found my job, I launched into my story. And every time someone told me they were job-hunting, I recommended they read *What Color Is Your Parachute?*

Job seekers called me at home and at work. After talking to them about creative job-hunting, I'd ask them to keep me posted on their progress--and they would. It became clear the approach was **even more helpful for people with disabilities** than for able-bodied people.

In a later article about Dick Bolles, the *Reader's Digest* featured me as a success story. Dick and I exchanged letters. I read each of his books, each version of *What Color Is Your Parachute?*, as it came out. The more I read, the more connected with him I felt. I sent him my books as well. About a decade later, still happily working at the job he helped me find, I read *Job-Hunting Tips for the So-Called Handicapped* and was impressed with its words of wisdom.[1]

Still another decade later, while researching *Learning a Living: A Career Guide for People with Learning Disabilities, Attention Deficit Disorder, and Dyslexia,* I ordered Dick's book for potential use in my resource directory. The book did seem to need updating. A lot had happened since he wrote it. The Americans with Disabilities Act had been passed, and his pioneering work on creative job-hunting had helped me mentor a lot of people. It was now clear how his techniques helped people with disabilities to get jobs. I felt a desire to work with him to create a new book, which covered ADA and gave a detailed explanation of how people with disabilities could use the "recipe" in *What Color Is Your Parachute?* The desire became stronger as time went on.

The 1998 edition of *What Color Is Your Parachute?* included Dick Bolles's name and address and a promise to read whatever readers wrote. So I wrote a letter offering to expand and update the book.

Writing him was a bit nerve-racking. I felt as if I knew him, but didn't know for sure he had read my letters or my books. It seemed possible that he barely knew me, and the possibility of being ignored and rejected scared me. But, despite my fears, I sent the letter off. Well, numerous letters, phone calls, faxes, FedEx packages, and conversations later, we

---

Footnote: A Personal Disclaimer
1. This book was written separately from my job. It was completed on my "own time" -- meaning evenings, weekends, and vacations. Clearly, it does not represent the official position of the President's Committee on Employment of People with Disabilities, the Department of Labor, or any other organization.

were ready to start our partnership. Feeling thrilled, I started rewriting this book and writing the new material for it!

My hopes for this book are that:

- It spreads the word about creative job-hunting throughout the rehabilitation community and that many more service providers will teach creative job-hunting skills, in addition to the traditional job-hunting skills they currently teach;
- It sparks a dialogue among people with disabilities about creative job-hunting;
- A lot of books and materials will now get written that will be very specific about how to improve our skills in searching for work. These should be high-quality, readable, interesting texts with ideas on how to cope with the problems each disability brings, and . . .
- Many more of us are successful in finding jobs.

My hope for you, if you are a reader with a disability, is that you will be successful in finding the job and career that makes you happy, passionate, and thrilled to go to work each morning. And that the process of finding work and then doing that job will overcome the thousands of unkind cuts that people can inflict on those with disabilities in our society.

People with disabilities have the highest unemployment rate of any group in our society. This is a disgrace! **Please help to change this the best way you can -- by finding a job yourself**. And if you are a counselor or parent or sister or brother or friend of a person with a disability, **help them find work --** and **expect** them to keep working at finding work that they love.

I truly believe for most of you the best way to do that is to use *What Color Is Your Parachute?* and possibly the *What Color Is Your Parachute? Workbook* plus this book . . . and take each step required to find a job that fulfills you.

The recommendations in this book will be easy to read.

The problem is that they only work if you do them--if you change them from thought to action. It is my hope that you gather your courage and determination and actually do what we suggest, for ideas can only help those who are willing to act on them. You must do the day-to-day work of job-hunting, and we ask you to do so.

Our society is going through a transformation in its attitudes toward people with disabilities--and there are more opportunities available. However, oppression and discrimination still exist. By joining the workforce, you are (1) setting an example for other people with disabilities; (2) showing nondisabled people what you (and, through you, other people with disabilities--and in particular with your disability) can do; and (3) becoming a part of a large-scale social movement in which people with disabilities are taking their rightful place in the economy.

That is also true if you are employed, but looking for a better job or a promotion where you work.

If you are now job-hunting and reading this book as part of your strategy, we hope you find **encouragement and helpful ideas**. If you haven't yet started, we hope you are inspired. We encourage you to take the first step (often the hardest) and many more thereafter.

So, as you read this book, please keep in mind that you will soon actually be **doing the work of looking for work**. Or to put it another way, you already have a job--the job of looking for a job. And know that we are with you all the way, cheering you on . . . and anticipating your success.

CHAPTER 1

A Short Course on Disabilities

FOR THOSE OF US WHO DO NOT (YET) HAVE A DISABILITY

The word "disability" is defined in many different ways. Ironically, the U.S. Census defines disability as *"a condition that limits or prevents working."* According to the latest published survey, 17.4 million people who are working age (16–64) had such a disability.[1]

Of course, that's a pretty bad definition. The government is trying to improve it, because so many people with severe disabilities do succeed in working. The very point of this book is that everyone is employable.

Another definition, from the Survey of Income and Program Participation (SIPP), includes more people. Of course, it covers people who are unable to work or limited in the work they can do. But, it also includes people qualified for Social Security, who use wheelchairs, who report limits in what they can do, and those with other specified conditions. When this broader definition was used, the SIPP found 32 million

---

1. Susan Stoddard, Lita Jans, Joan M. Ripple, and Lewis Kraus, *Chartbook on Work and Disability in the United States, 1998,* an InfoUse Report (Washington, DC: U.S. National Institute on Disability and Rehabilitation Research, 1998), 7.

working-age people with disabilities.[2] The SIPP defined "working age" as 15–64.

Vocabulary is very important to all of us with disabilities. Generalizations are difficult to make, because vocabulary is hotly debated even within the disability community. But *as a general rule*, people with disabilities prefer to call themselves "people" or "people with disabilities," thus making each one **a person primarily** and one with a disability secondarily. "Disabled" is second on the list of preferred terms. Unfortunately many employers think of "disabled workers" as people who are out on workers' compensation.

"Handicapped" has come into great disfavor, although it does remain, in some public signs. The reason it is not liked is because of the history of the word. Veterans of the Crimean War used to beg with their cap in their hands. So, the term "handicapped" came to be.

People who use wheelchairs do not like the terminology "confined to a wheelchair," because many can transfer out of their chair to another seat or can use crutches. In addition, they feel a wheelchair liberates them from staying home. People with mental retardation prefer the term "cognitively disabled" or "self-advocate." People with psychiatric disabilities vary in the terminology they like. Some common ones include "mental health client," "consumer of mental health services," "mental health disability," and "psychiatric system survivor."[3] People who cannot see, generally prefer to be called "people who are blind," though some do like the term "the blind." Some who can see a little prefer "visually impaired," "partially sighted," or "print impaired." People who

---

2. Ibid., 4.

3. Well-known advocate for people with psychiatric disabilities Laura Mancuso, author of *Case Studies of Reasonable Accommodations for Workers with Psychiatric Disabilities,* was the source of several of these terms in a voice-mail message to the author of this book on February 24, 1999.

are deaf come in two groups. Some people who are deaf consider themselves part of the "deaf culture." They use the term "Deaf" with a capital D. This refers to the group of people that communicates primarily through American Sign Language. Many of them are deaf children born in deaf families. Gallaudet University in Washington, DC, is a center of the "deaf culture."[4] Those people who cannot hear but are not in the Deaf culture say they are "people who are deaf" or that they "can't hear." Other people who cannot hear well but have some hearing prefer "a person with a hearing impairment."

About 36 percent of men with disabilities who are of working age (16–64 years) are in the labor force or *actively seeking work* and for women with disabilities, that figure is 30 percent.[5] That means that 64 percent of the men and 70 percent of the women are not in the labor force. These latter figures are often quoted as the unemployment rate among people with disabilities, though technically one is unemployed only if one *wants* to work and cannot find a job despite looking for one. Nonetheless, even with some allowance for this fact, people with disabilities remain **the group with by far the highest unemployment rate in the United States today**. A Harris Poll showed that seven out of ten people with disabilities who are not working do want to work.[6] This, of course, represents an untapped labor pool that employers desperately need, in order to fill the many open jobs in today's economy. No matter how the labor market changes, the United States needs the skills and talents of all of its citizens.

Before this untapped **labor pool** of people with disabilities

---

4. Antonio Eades from the public relations office of Gallaudet University confirmed this information in a phone call to Dale S. Brown on February 15, 1999.

5. Stoddard et al., *Chartbook on Work and Disability*, 13.

6. *1998 N.O.D./Harris Survey of Americans with Disabilities*, conducted by Louis Harris and Associates, Inc., commissioned by the National Organization on Disability (New York: Louis Harris & Associates, 1998), 44.

can be utilized, employers will have to discard many of the myths they believe without thinking, such as "People who are retarded are great at single-step repetitious tasks, and they don't mind doing them." Or, "People with quadriplegia are naturally good computer programmers." Or, "He's disabled--so he can't work here. We are too high pressure." Forty-two percent of people with disabilities say that an important reason they aren't working is because employers won't recognize that they are capable of doing a full-time job despite their disability or health problem.[7]

Consider the kinds of jobs people with disabilities actually hold. Let's take people who are blind as an example. The full-time jobs they hold down include artists, auto mechanics, ballerinas, beekeepers, bicycle repair people, boatbuilders, carpenters, chiropractors, college professors, counselors (drug/alcohol/youth/marriage), court reporters, dispatchers for 911 transportation companies, finger painters, fish-cleaners, food service managers, inventors, lawyers, licensed practical nurses, machinists, managers of snack stands and cafeterias in federal and other government buildings, marketing specialists, massage therapists, medical and legal transcribers, models (on runways as well as for magazines), musicians, packagers/assemblers in all kinds of manufacturing, painters, peanut vendors in stands at basketball or football games, professional storytellers, psychiatrists, public relations professionals, sculptors, strippers, teachers, word-processing and data-entry people, writers--and various kinds of self-employment. And this is only a sampling.

What kinds of salaries do people with disabilities make? Well in 1994–95, male workers with severe disabilities who were working full-time earned $1,262 a month. Those who did not have a disability earned $2,190 a month. Women with

---

7. Ibid., 46.

severe disabilities earned $1,000 a month. Those who had no disability earned $1,470 a month.[8]

A survey in which people with disabilities were questioned about their earnings showed that:

- 33 percent of people with disabilities who work make $25,000 or less a year;
- 40 percent make between $25,001 and $50,000 a year; and
- 20 percent make more than $50,001.[9]

While the average *salary earned* may seem respectable, it must be weighed against economic disincentives for ever going to work that confront a person once they have a disability and are receiving some sort of disability payments from a former employer or government, state or federal. These disincentives include:

- **The loss of sizable medical insurance** that they may have been receiving from state/federal programs (e.g., SSDI --Social Security Disability Insurance, or SSI--Supplemental Security Income), though the recent passage of The Ticket to Work and Work Incentives Improvement Act of 1999 may ameliorate this problem in the future.

- **The inability to get similar insurance from one's new employer,** since most private insurance companies will not cover preexisting conditions.

- **The mandatory time gap of up to two years a person faces** between the time one may lose a job (due to "downsizing," "hostile takeovers," or being fired) and the time that one's old state/federal medical insurance can be reinstated.

Other factors include the need for **time off for medical treatment** (69 percent), the need for **equipment or special**

---

8. Stoddard et al., *Chartbook on Work and Disability*, 24.
9. *1998 N.O.D./Harris Survey of Americans with Disabilities*, 37. Numbers do not add up to 100 due to computer rounding errors.

devices (28 percent), **and the lack of convenient and accessible transportation** (24 percent).[10] Also, some workplaces are still **inaccessible**, even though it is usually illegal. This happens despite the tax incentives to help small businesses that want to develop access.

What all of this adds up to is that a person with a disability may receive less total income (including medical payments) if they go to work than if they stay home. Nonetheless, people with disabilities *still* elect to seek work, even when it is economically disadvantageous for them to do so--even as people from "the private sector" may go into government service despite a similar loss of income. When people with disabilities do so, at such great personal cost, it is usually because of their driving need to put their God-given abilities into the service of the world. And, because of their need to maintain or increase their own sense of self-worth, as well as to prevent their skills from deteriorating through disuse.

It is certainly to our nation's advantage to assure that each person with a disability is employed inasmuch as the costs to the nation of their *not* working are:

- the loss of taxes they would otherwise pay;
- the loss of the money they would otherwise put into the economy through their **purchases** of life's necessities;
- the loss of **family income and taxes**, where family members are forced to take part-time work or give up work all together; and
- the cost of **government funds** to support the unemployed person who has a disability.

While throughout this book, we will be speaking of "people with disabilities" as though they are one "tribe," there is in actual fact, no such thing as a *typical* disabled person. As experts point out, every disability is a mix of three things:

10. Ibid., 46.

No Two Disabled Persons Are Alike

Each One is a PERSON who has a disability
that has one of the characteristics on each line below:*

HIDDEN		VISIBLE	
i.e., not immediately apparent to others		i.e., immediately or quickly apparent to others	

MILD	MODERATE	SEVERE	PROFOUND

CONGENITAL		ADVENTITIOUS	
i.e., it occurred either at birth or before they were 5		i.e., it came (*advent*) into their life after they were 5	

Their impairment only limits their ability to:

SEE	HEAR	SPEAK	MOVE	THINK OR LEARN	FEEL OR BEHAVE	OTHER	More than one of the previous

With respect to their abilities in other areas:

THEY ARE NORMALLY GIFTED	THEY ARE EXTRAORDINARILY GIFTED
in other areas	in one or more other areas

Their attitude toward their disability is:

THEY SEE IT AS A DISASTER	THEY SEE IT AS A CHALLENGE
that has overwhelmed them	for them to overcome

Their driving motive in life (*besides survival*) is their desire for:

AFFILIATION	ACHIEVEMENT	EXCELLING
or the need to relate to people	or the need to outdo their own record	or the need to outdo others

In dealing with their disability they are:

SOCIALLY ISOLATED	SOCIALLY SUPPORTED
hence, dealing with it essentially on their own	hence, dealing with it with help from others

In dealing with their **abilities** they are:

UNAWARE	WELL AWARE
of what they can do, and do well, and enjoy	of what they can do, and do well, and enjoy

*N.B. The categories on one line are NOT necessarily related to the categories immediately below it.

An Impairment (the actual limitations caused by the disability), **The Individual** (their personality, attitude, resources, etc.), and **The Environment** (how friendly or barring it is to that disability, how much support it offers to that individual). The outcome of that mix will vary widely from one person with a disability to another. The chart on the facing page, however, shows *something* of the immense varieties of disability.

Not mentioned in the chart are the varying *causes* of any specific disability. For example, if we see someone using a wheelchair, their "impairment of motion" may be due to amputation after an auto accident, arthritis, cerebral palsy, epilepsy, muscular dystrophy, polio, spina bifida, spinal cord injuries, or a variety of other causes.

What do these varying causes signify? They signify that disability is not like race, or height, or your birthplace. Where you were born will always be where you were born. Your race and height will also not change. But whether or not you are one of "the so-called handicapped or disabled" can change during the next twenty-four hours. This is why people with disabilities sometimes call everyone else TABs -- for "temporarily able-bodied."

Five out of every six people with disabilities were NOT born with that disability. New causes of disability are constantly appearing; among those in the news recently include AIDS, chronic fatigue syndrome, children of mothers who take crack cocaine, attention deficit disorder, and carpal tunnel syndrome.

All of us, therefore, are only one incident or microbe away from joining this group of "people with disabilities." You can become permanently disabled with one accident at home, one fall (on an icy step, on a slippery sidewalk, on a newly waxed floor, down a flight of stairs, off a ladder, off a roof, on a ski slope, on an amateur playing field), one unexpected crippling

illness (arthritis, heart disease, among others), one auto accident, one encounter with the wrong insect, or virus, or chemical agent. And this book, which you read today out of
curiosity or compassion for others, may tomorrow become
words you need for your very own life.

CHAPTER 2

The Americans with Disabilities Act

WHAT IT CAN DO--AND WHAT IT CANNOT DO

T he Americans with Disabilities Act (ADA), signed by
President George Bush in 1990, was a major step forward for people with disabilities. It gave people with disabilities civil rights--much like the ones held by minorities and
women. The ADA covers transportation, public accommodations such as stores and hotels, telecommunications, and, of
course, employment. The ADA makes it **illegal** for employers
to discriminate against you because you have a disability.

And it has helped **some** people with disabilities get and
keep jobs. Approximately 800,000 more severely disabled individuals were working in 1994 than in 1991 according to the
Census Bureau's Survey of Income Program and Participation (SIPP).[1]

We thought the legislation would be our knight in shining
armor, riding to our rescue on a dazzling white steed. We
thought that knight would guarantee us jobs. Well, the knight
has indeed come along--except the armor is tarnished and
the horse needs a good wash.

---

1. "Employment Rate of People with Disabilities Increases under the
Americans with Disabilities Act," President's Committee on Employment
of People with Disabilities, Washington, DC, news release, July 22, 1996.

Much like a knight on a white horse, there are things the ADA can do for us--and things that it cannot do for us. This chapter will begin to describe what it can do--as well as what we must do for ourselves.

WHAT THE ADA CAN DO FOR US

The Americans with Disabilities Act stated officially that people with disabilities experienced discrimination and tried to address that discrimination. It was passed by a massive effort of people with disabilities. They showed the nation (including many employers) that we were capable of organizing ourselves to pass a law.

Before the ADA passed, business owners could refuse to serve us in restaurants or not let us stay in a hotel. A grocery store clerk could refuse to take groceries down from high shelves--even if that meant a customer with a disability then could not shop there.

It is hard to believe that before the ADA passed, applications had long lists of disabilities and health conditions. The job seeker had to check off those that they had--and these check marks were sometimes used to throw out the forms and not even interview those people.

No employer can look at us straight in the eye and say, "I am sorry, but we don't hire blind people." Or, "You have learning disabilities. So, we aren't willing to promote you." Or, "We don't pay for training for people who are deaf. It's just too expensive."

These things were said in the past--and the ADA has almost ended that era of blatant oppression.

The passage of the ADA--and the activities to publicize the law and make it work--awakened the conscience of many employers. They also became aware of the loss to their companies because of discrimination. They realized that they were missing out on valuable workers--and became determined to assure that everyone who was qualified could compete for jobs in their company. They also saw that they were losing money when good, experienced people went out on disability instead of producing on the job.

The Americans with Disabilities Act has rules (some legal and complicated and still wending their way through various levels of court) that set up a fair competition for each open job with employers that have fifteen or more employees. It basically covers announced openings where applicants are selected in a competitive manner. During the job interview, the employer may not ask you whether you have a disability or ask questions about your disability, unless you bring it up yourself (often a good idea if your disability is visible). Employers can give medical exams, only after they have made a job offer. And then, all people who received offers for the same type of employment would have to take the exam.

The Americans with Disabilities Act says that you have a right to "reasonable accommodation." The term "reasonable accommodation" refers to changes in how the job is done, the equipment you use, and the way people communicate with you. These changes, if made, will prevent your disability from being a barrier to securing a job and doing high-quality work once you are employed. Reasonable accommodation might also keep your disability from interfering with your efforts to fill out an application or participate in an interview.

It is a myth that "accommodating" the job is only done for people with disabilities. Jobs have been and are changed and accommodated all the time for many people. However, many workers with visible disabilities and health conditions had trouble persuading employers to accommodate them. Some were fired unfairly. So the law was needed to make accommodation a right rather than a privilege.

Some examples of accommodation include:

• Interpreters for people who are deaf
• Readers for people who are blind

- Equipment that enlarges print so it is easier to read
- A specialized keyboard that makes it possible to type with one hand on a computer
- Schedule changes that make it possible to care for yourself within the medical regimen required by your disability

When you are competing for a job, the ADA can help you perform well in the interview. For example, if you are a deaf person interviewing at a large company, you can request an interpreter -- and probably have the company provide one.

WHAT THE ADA CANNOT DO FOR US

The ADA has spawned a number of myths -- incorrect beliefs among some people with disabilities, their counselors, their parents, and their friends -- about what the law says. These myths have done us grave damage. They raise expectations that cannot be met and encourage an attitude of entitlement rather than effort.

The first myth: The ADA gives us special privileges.

It does not. A misunderstanding of the right of reasonable accommodation by some people has created the myth. The ADA gives us the right to *reasonable* accommodation. The important word here is "reasonable." *You* might think that a particular accommodation is reasonable. But *the employer* might think it is unreasonable.

Reasonable accommodation requires negotiation between you and the employer. The employer does not have to give you an accommodation if they can prove it is an "undue hardship," which means it is too expensive or too difficult. Employers have the right to request medical documentation of your disability -- and the need for the accommodation.

And, they are only responsible for the "known" disability of the applicant. So, if you have a hidden disability, you must disclose it to be covered. You have to decide if you want to disclose it during the interview when you are competing against other applicants (rarely a good idea in our opinion), after you have the offer (a slightly better idea), or after you are on the job. Each of these options has advantages and disadvantages. But, the point we are making is this--if you want to keep information about your disability to yourself, you miss much of the benefit of the ADA.

Basically, you have the right to accommodation that brings you to the starting line, that enables you to do the job despite problems caused by your disability. You do not have the right to an accommodation that gives you anything extra. So you can have a change in schedule that allows you to take your medication with the proper timing of doses, but you cannot come in whenever you feel like it. You probably have the right to get instructions repeated to you several times, but you do not have the right to a "patient boss." You can get some extra secretarial help--but not necessarily the best secretary. Basically, you only get what you need to perform the job at the same level as a nondisabled person.

The second myth: The ADA guarantees us a job.

It does not. A hard-core group of people with disabilities honestly believes that a given employer must hire them because of the ADA. **This is not true**. Nobody in the United States is guaranteed a job. All of us must find an employer who wants to hire someone and persuade that employer that we are the right someone. This myth has done significant damage to some people. Convinced the ADA entitles them to a job, they do not prepare themselves well for interviews, they do not do their homework, they are not courteous during job interviews, they call people in nonprofit agencies and in the government and demand jobs. They need to read this book and learn that they must earn a job--just like everyone else. And

32

also like everyone else, they must learn that they are not entitled to a job.

The third myth: The ADA might give us a few extra points in the competition to get a job.

It does not. The ADA only covers *qualified* people with disabilities. So, even though it is harder for people with disabilities to become well educated and get on-the-job experience, the ADA gives employers the right to refuse employment to people who do not have the correct qualifications. Of course, the employer is not allowed to invent qualifications to screen out people with disabilities. So, if a driver's license is required, for example, the employer has to show that driving is important to the job. On the other hand, if you want to work as a doctor, you must have a medical degree. If the job calls for five years of experience doing X, then you must have five years of doing X. The creative job-hunting approach detailed in this book gets you around artificial qualifications in cases where you are the right person for the job. Again, the ADA gets you to the starting line, but it does not move you ahead in the race.

The fourth myth: The ADA has ended discrimination.

It has not. It has lessened discrimination by making it illegal. But some employers, determined to "beat the law," just decided to be a lot more subtle. For example, preemployment tests have become a legal way to locate individuals with disabilities. You are allowed to ask for reasonable accommodation to take the test. But, if you have difficulty reading, trouble sitting for long periods of time, mild hearing loss, or any challenge in taking tests, you must reveal this to the employer while you are still in competition with other people.

True, as mentioned earlier, employers may not ask you about your disability. But some employers' search firms ask applicants to sign release forms, allowing them to check your credit history, leave records, information from schools you attended, past employers, personal references, and who knows what else--information that might unwittingly reveal your disability, before they ever decide if they will grant you an interview.

In addition, discrimination is very difficult to prove. If your disability is visible, then a job interview can cause you to be screened out if the interviewer feels uneasy with your disability. Since a large number of other candidates are interviewed, you will be unable to prove that the cause of your rejection was discrimination.

And should you try to prove it through a lawsuit, you may find that the courts have not been friendly to the ADA. The Supreme Court has found that people may not be truly disabled under the ADA if they take medication or if in any other way their disability is mitigated. Some lawyers have argued successfully that employees did not document their disability well enough. Attorneys have come up with many creative rationales to disprove ADA cases. And, so, the sorry results: nine out of ten cases have been won by employers.[2]

LEGAL ACTION: HOW DO YOU PROCEED?

What if you want to consider legal action anyway? To look into that possibility, study the Americans with Disabilities Act. Your public library probably has a great deal of information. Also try these information sources.

U.S. Equal Employment Opportunity Commission (EEOC)

1801 L Street NW
Washington, DC 20507
Phone: 800-669-4000 (for questions about employment

---

2. "ABA Study Shows Employers Win Most Disability Discrimination Suits," news release, American Bar Association, June 16, 1998.

provisions or office locations); 800-669-6820 (TTY) 800-669-3362 (to order documents); 800-800-3302 (TTY) Web site: http://www.eeoc.gov

The EEOC is willing to explain the ADA provisions that apply to employment and also will explain how to file a complaint.

The Disability Rights Education and Defense Fund (DREDF) ADA Hotline
800-466-4232 (Voice/TTY)

This hotline provides information about the Americans with Disabilities Act and specializes in the issues of people with disabilities themselves.

Filing a lawsuit or a complaint is a major step. It should not be taken lightly. It will consume time and money. And, law works by precedent. If you lose your complaint, similar complaints in the future are likely to be lost. (Of course, if you win, similar complaints in the future are likely to be won.) So, if your case is solid and well grounded, your victory could help other people with disabilities.

But this is not a book about advocacy for other people with disabilities. It is a book about getting a job that you love. Will you love a job where you have to work for someone who you just sued?

The time and money that you spend on legal battles is time and money taken away from your job-hunt. It may keep you from doing the thorough research, meeting with employers, and doing the other steps of seeking work.

The reality is that even with ADA, job-hunting will be a huge challenge for you--as it is for everyone. And, although ADA does give you some new "rights," you will find that "rights" don't necessarily help you get the "right" job. They might prevent an employer from discriminating against you, but, in general, the way the world works, **nobody has to hire** you. All they have to do is to find a good reason, based on business necessity, to hire someone else or leave the job open.

Your best bet is to find a problem you can solve, a situation where your skills and talents are needed, and an employer who is willing to hire you. In short, find a job.

So, the question is, in view of all that we have discussed--what we have and do not have with the ADA--what is the best way to get a job? That is what the rest of this book is about.

CHAPTER 3

Job-Hunting and People
with Disabilities

When it comes to getting a job, in some ways, your task is basically the same task faced by a person who does not have any disability. You are a person with strengths and talents to share. You must find ways to communicate those abilities to people who are able to hire you. Yet, in other ways your task is very different. For example, there **is** a group of employers that you **must** avoid.

Employers divide into two groups. The first group consists of those who will be bothered by your disability or will rigidly stick to the job requirements exactly as they are and refuse any exception because of your disability. The second group consists of those who won't be bothered with your disability. Or they are a little bothered, but are enlightened enough to realize their feelings might be irrational -- and are willing to try to treat you fairly. They **will** hire you so long as you can do the job.

Your task is to **find** the second group of employers and just thank the first very politely for their time, plus secure any referrals they might give. Fortunately, there are more employers in the second group than ever before. But, the employers in the first group, those who discriminate against you, will make your job-hunt more difficult.

Another problem, if you are working already, is that **your own employer** might be in that first group! If you have just become disabled, your own employer whom you worked for faithfully may try to get you to retire on disability. Or might try to cancel your job while you are recovering.

If that happens, do everything you can to persuade your employer that you are eager to stay employed. Set a date when you might return. Ask to work a little bit while you are recovering. Call your friends at work and ask them for the latest news. And show an interest in the office. If things get adversarial, focus with your attorney and the union, if you have one, on **staying** on the job rather than on **leaving** the job and maximizing your disability benefits.

Another situation: Let's suppose you are a person with a disability and you have worked at a place for, say, five years. Things are going well and your disability is not an issue. Then, something changes that makes your disability an issue when it wasn't before.

Say, for example, that you had a flexible starting time -- nobody really cared whether you came in at 8:30 or 9:15 in the morning. But now, there's been a tardiness crackdown, and sometimes -- at unpredictable intervals -- you have to spend an hour dealing with a self-care issue relating to your disability. Or, you get a promotion -- and now there is three times as much reading and writing. You could handle it before, but your dyslexia is a problem now.

You might try working with your employer to get an accommodation to your disability. If you are reading this book because you are unhappy on the job -- and the reason you are unhappy is discrimination -- take the time and effort to look at the reason you are unhappy and address it with your supervisor. You might be able to keep your job and enjoy it for many years more. If you don't succeed, and don't want to sue your employer to stay, you will need to search for another job. Which is what this book is all about.

So, back to job-hunting.

For the typical job-hunter, the hunt goes like this:

No
  No
   No
    No
     Yes, oops, the salary is half of what I deserve.
      No
       No
        No
         No
          No
           Maybe, oh darn, the job was canceled.
         No
         No
          No
          No
            They say, "We'll call you," but they don't call.
  No
   No
    No
     No
      No
       Yes

For you, the job-hunt will have more "No's" before the "Yes," and will include:

Yes - - oh, darn it, our computer equipment just can't be changed to fit your adaptive device.

Yes - - but we require forty hours a week of attendance, 9:00 A.M.–5:30 P.M. - - Well let's face it, doctor's appointments will be a **big** problem.

But, if you are persistent, there will be a final **yes**.

REJECTION SHOCK

For almost every job-hunter, constant rejection often causes a condition of paralysis and depression. We call it "rejection shock." Your self-image plummets. You feel like something is wrong with you. Resume after resume has gone out. You have followed the rules. You have made sure that every cover letter is carefully aimed toward the person it is written to. And, there are no calls -- or interviews. You simply hear nothing.

Unfortunately, this **rejection** shock can be worse for a person with a disability, because most of us with long-term disabilities have already experienced terrible **rejection**. We may have been **rejected** by our playmates when we were young because of how we looked. We may have already been through major struggles getting into college or graduate school because the admissions committee **tried** to reject us. A lot of us have sat across from counselors and teachers who told us that **our disability prevented us from XXXX (which often was our dream**), instead of helping us figure out how the dream could be realized. Some adults whose disabilities start from accidents or disease lose their friends or even their spouse after their injury or illness. Some of us have been stared at because our disability startles people. To say nothing of the rejecting message implicit in inaccessible buildings, and Web sites or documents that we can't read. Handling this constant rejection from society -- and its impact on us -- is the subject of a separate chapter in our book (chapter 5), where we talk about handling internalized oppression. For now, we want to go directly to where you probably want to go:

THE TRUTH ABOUT JOB-HUNTING

You see, the real problem is our job-hunting system, the system that you were taught was the way to look for a job. Basically "the system" involves looking only for "openings" and then competing with others for them. Or sending your resume out to employers and hoping they call you. OK, things have changed. Now, you are encouraged to post your resume on the Internet as well as mail thousands of them to employers. You are taught what we call "the numbers game."

THE NUMBERS GAME AND HOW IT WORKS AGAINST PEOPLE WITH DISABILITIES

The numbers game works on the principle that employers should attract a large number of applicants, then screen a lot of them out, and then pick the best. The hidden goal of screening people out works against people with anything unusual about them--including, of course, people with disabilities.

The numbers game is frequently presented as the only game in town. Most books on job-hunting explain this system. Most job-hunting classes teach this system. The disability community, through its system of providing services, also teaches this system extensively.

Let's look at each step of the numbers game, used by most employers in the United States, and then consider how it works against those of us with disabilities.

> *The employer advertises for the position and collects as many resumes or applications as possible.*

This discriminates against **anyone whose disability (or for that matter, set of skills) makes it difficult for them to write or look good on paper.** So everyone who has poor handwriting or difficulty following directions on a computer screen, or difficulty writing a concise, interesting paragraph, or difficulty putting together a professional looking resume . . . is screened out.

The numbers game also discriminates against **those whose disability has made it difficult for them to gain a partic-**

ular "education" or "years-of-experience" type of qual-
ification--even, if these qualifications aren't *really* necessary
to do the job they are seeking. People without those qualifications . . . are screened out.

Another thing: you will often be required to describe your
career sequentially. Unless you find a way to hide it, this discriminates against **anyone who has a gap in their employment record**. So . . . if you were, say, hospitalized for a mental
or physical illness for a year . . . or on benefits for three
years . . . you will be . . . screened out.

> ### The employer conducts initial interviews to see
> ### who they want to seriously consider for the job.

These interviews are often for the purpose of **screening out**
unsuitable applicants. There are many ways of screening out
people: preemployment tests, asking questions and screening
out people who don't answer a certain way, studying one's
reaction to a person's physical appearance, or even the "gut
feeling" of the interviewer.

If your disability is visible, the interview can cause you to
be screened out if the interviewer feels uneasy with your disability. But since a large number of other candidates are interviewed, you will be unable to prove that the cause of your
rejection is discrimination.

> ### Then, there is a finalist interview in which you
> ### finally get to talk to the person with the power
> ### to hire you.

At this point, you have overcome most of the barriers the
numbers game as put in your way. The only problem that
you have to worry about that is unique to your disability is
the possibility that your interviewer may see your disability
and not you. Your disability might make your prospective
boss nervous, if they are part of the first group of employers

who are simply bothered by disability. But, the numbers game makes it very unlikely you will get to this point.

In short, because the system is set up so that screening people out is the way the employer "wins" . . . and because of the large number of applicants that come in response to hiring announcements, you will frequently be rejected the same way everyone else gets rejected in this process. To top it off, you may also be discriminated against--and in a given situation, there is no definite way to figure out why the employer hired someone else.

THE CREATIVE JOB-HUNTING TECHNIQUE

The numbers game causes so much difficulty for applicants with disabilities that we wanted to present an alternative strategy to you. That is why we wrote this book. The alternative strategy is described in detail in the book *What Color Is Your Parachute?* We call it "creative job-hunting." It works better for most job-hunters than the traditional ways of looking, which encompass the worst ways to find a job. They are:

• Using the Internet to search job postings
• Mailing resumes to employers
• Answering ads announcing vacancies
• Going to private employment agencies or search firms

The creative job-hunt is one of the five best ways to find a job. The five best ways are:

• Asking for job leads from people you know or meet
• Visiting employers (J. Michael Farr, President of JIST Publishing and well-known career author, has defined a job interview as a meeting with anyone that hires people for the type of job you want, whether or not there is an opening at the time of your discussion.)

- Calling employers from the Yellow Pages or other directories and asking them if they are hiring for your position
- Doing this in a group with other job-hunters
- The creative approach, which has an 86 percent success rate

The creative approach involves the following steps:

- Know your skills.
- Know what kind of work you want to do.
- Talk to the people who are doing it.
- Find out how they like the work and how they found their job.
- Do some research, in your chosen geographical area, on organizations that interest you.
- Find out what they do and what kind of problems they or their industry are wrestling with.
- Identify or seek out the person who actually has the power to hire you for the job you want.
- Use your contacts to get in to see them.
- Show this person how you can help them with their problems and how you would stand out as one employee in a hundred.

That's the method used by all creative job-seekers. (We'll explore this method more fully below.) Of course, you have a disability. You face discrimination. OK, then, you will have to show them how you would stand out as one employee in two hundred.

HANDLING YOUR DISABILITY WHILE YOU LOOK FOR WORK THE CREATIVE WAY

We believe the best way to do this is through the creative job-hunting process. If it is done properly, it can minimize your disability as an issue. You are looking for a person or group of people who will hire you for what you love to do and what you are good at. Period. When you find people who discriminate against you, you will sweetly and politely avoid them -- unless, of course, they can help you find the people who **won't** discriminate against you.

However, as in all activities of life, your disability must be addressed. This section gives you some ways of doing so. Each step of the creative job-hunting process is described in detail in *What Color Is Your Parachute?* Our short way of describing the steps is: **What, Where, and How.** Let's describe each step, then discuss how to handle your disability.

Step 1: What Do You Want to Do? The prescription: A **thorough** evaluation of your strengths and weaknesses. Which of your skills do you most delight in using? What are your talents? What do you really want to do? Look for work that you only **think** you should do and you probably won't look very hard. But look for work that you **deeply want**, and you'll probably look with **all of your soul** -- and end up finding it.

Step 2: Where Do You Want to Do It? The prescription: You must decide **where** you want to use your skills. You must decide:

- What subjects interest you, for instance, medicine, politics, gardening
- Where you want to live
- What knowledge you know already that you want to use, i.e., how to budget, how to repair small appliances, how to improve computer software, etc.
- Your preferred working conditions, such as need for autonomy or direction, a preference for variety or routine, etc.

- What jobs exist that use your skills and combine the things you love to do
- What organizations have such jobs

To figure all of this out, you will need to do a lot of research, both written (visiting Internet sites and libraries) and oral (talking to people on the telephone and in person). We recommend informational interviews as the best way to find out what you need to know. You use such interviews to:

- Talk to people who have the career or job you want (or think you want). Ask questions to find out if you would like it, how to prepare yourself, what the job requires day-to-day, and how they like each activity. If possible, find someone with a disability like your own -- or at least another disability.

- Learn about trends, organizations that might hire you, organizations that recently received grants or any infusion of cash, organizations that might use your skills, details about a potential place you might want to work, and any information that helps you determine the fit between your skills and a potential way of making a living.

- Build relationships with the best of the people you interview. Find ways to contribute to their goals and become known in the field.

Step 3: How Do You Obtain Such a Job? The prescription: Go to the organizations that interest you the most whether or not they have a vacancy. Use your contacts to get an interview there. Know the needs of the person with the power to hire you. Show you are the one who can solve their problems and make their job easier.

OK, that is the process in a nutshell. Now, let's discuss how your disability will impact each of these activities. We'll go step by step.

Step 1: What Do You Want to Do?

Thoroughly evaluate your passion and your skills. Determine your mission in life. What would you do even if you weren't paid?

Here are some challenges that people with disabilities often have with this step and some possible solutions.

▶ **Challenge:**

You have low self-esteem as a result of the oppression and discrimination that you have faced. So many people have told you what you **can't** do, it is hard to focus on what you **can** do.

▶ **Responses:**

1. Realize that you owe it to yourself to find work that you are passionate about.
2. Join groups of people that will encourage you to take pride in yourself--that means your whole self, including the parts of yourself some people think of as disabled and devalued. Find positive people and make friends with them.
3. Rigorously work at identifying your strengths. Review your life **thoroughly** and write a **long** list of strengths with a lot of supporting examples. Remember, there are many, many books that describe how to do that in your library and bookstore. Attend career seminars in your community.
4. Talk back to the negative voices in your head. For example, suppose you find yourself thinking, "I don't have any strengths." Reply strongly, "Of course I have strengths." Then name them. The effort you put into identifying your talents will pay off here.
5. Ask yourself questions that will raise your self-esteem. For example, at the end of each day, you might ask:
   • What did I learn today that will help my job-hunt?
   • In what ways did I show employers that I would make a good employee?
   • When was I really working hard and effectively?

47

6. Remember, **the key to self-esteem is self-discipline and action** that brings you closer to your goals. **Plan your work and work your plan**. Decide what you are going to do and do it. Even if you do not get a job as fast as you wish you would, you will find your developing self-control makes you feel wonderful about yourself.
7. Chapter 5 has many helpful recommendations for low self-esteem.
8. If you are stuck on this step, go to a career counselor, either a rehabilitation counselor or a counselor who works with many types of job seekers. We will discuss this later on page 115.

► **Challenge:**

You don't realize that you have a certain skill, because your disabilities were not accommodated and thus the skill did not develop normally. Or you have a skill, but your disabilities make it difficult for you and other people to recognize it.

Examples:
• You have learning disabilities and have great difficulty with spelling and grammar. You are a good writer, but have received so many papers with red marks on them, you think you are a poor writer.
• You use a wheelchair, have great physical coordination, stamina, and strength. However, you have never had the opportunity to play on sports teams for athletes who use wheelchairs, and think of yourself as weak and uncoordinated.
• You were a successful artist when you became blind. Your rehabilitation counselor told you that you had to change fields. You did not know about the Job Accommodation Network, VSA Arts, or other resources that could teach you how you could continue your art, with accommodations for your blindness.

▶ **Responses:**

1. When you list your skills and think about what you enjoy doing, be very inclusive. Do not leave out possible strengths because they seem too minor or small, because they are not noticed or encouraged, or because you are not sure they are real strengths.

2. Write or tell stories about what you enjoy doing and do well. Find two other people and work in a group. Each of you reads a story. Then the other people listen and list the skills that were illustrated.

▶ **Challenge:**

Everybody says you would be perfect as a "role model" and you should work with people who have your disability.

▶ **Response:**

Realize this reaction probably has nothing to do with you as an individual. It is part of the pattern of segregating people with disabilities. Of course, if you believe it **is** your mission to work with other people with disabilities, you should do it. As a matter of fact, one of the authors of the book (Dale Brown) spent twenty years leading the self-help movement for people with learning disabilities. But most people who have disabilities have other interests that have **nothing** to do with their disability. Tell the well-meaning "admirers" that you will be a great role model as soon as you find a job in the field that interests you.

▶ **Challenge:**

Most of the skill identification exercises in *What Color Is Your Parachute?* (and the *What Color Is Your Parachute? Workbook*) or in other resources you might use involve writing down your thoughts. Your disability makes that very difficult.

► **Responses:**

1. Talk into a tape recorder as you think through the exercises.

2. Get a friend, family member, or counselor to serve as your "listening partner." These are the steps you follow:

   a. Explain to them that you are trying to determine what you are good at and that you need them to listen to you and take notes as you talk. Tell them that you don't need advice. What you need is a sounding board, someone who will respectfully hear you.

   b. Have them ask you the questions or give you the directions from the exercises.

   c. Talk to them, thinking aloud.

   d. Ask them for a copy of their notes. You may also ask them to highlight the places where you were the most enthusiastic. You can thus use a listening partner with any exercise that otherwise requires writing.

► **Challenge:**

You have been given glowing but false positive feedback. You have been told you were good at things that in fact you did poorly. This may happen for two reasons.

One is that the able-bodied world does not expect much of people with disabilities, particularly when these disabilities are visible. Students who have been in special education classrooms particularly suffer from low expectations. When people expect low quality from you, everything "good" will be considered excellent. So, let's say you are the best in your "special class." You are told you are incredible. But you are not informed that, compared to others your age, you are basically average.

The second reason that people give you glowing feedback (which is actually a good reason) is simply to encourage you. As you work in your area of weakness, giving you praise as you improve can indeed be helpful. The problem is that this is often done without giving you the information you would need to move your performance up to a higher level.

▶ **Responses:**

Share your ideas about your strengths with people who know you. Ask them for **very** honest feedback. Say, "I need this information to choose the right career--*please tell me the truth.*"

(People with disabilities are not the only ones with this problem. A recent study showed that people who scored in the lowest quarter on tests of logic, English grammar, and humor were the most likely to grossly exaggerate how well they scored on the test.[1])

The key to handling the "disability halo" is to make every effort to see yourself as others see you--and realize that how you perceive yourself might or might not be the truest reality.

Step 2: Where Do You Want to Do It?

The next step is to figure out **where** you want to use your skills. This refers not only to **where in the world** you want to work, but also to **what kind of organization and what kind of people** you want to work with.

This requires **written and oral** research--and you will go back and forth between these two kinds of research, using the one that will best help you find the information that you need.

You might start with written research, by going on Web sites and reading books to learn more about a particular division of a company. Then you realize that there are some major missing pieces of information--or that your various sources contradict each other on a key point. You "smell"

---

1. "Incompetent People Really Have No Idea, Studies Find," *San Francisco Chronicle,* January 18, 2000, A1.

The Job Accommodation Network (JAN)

As you work on creative job-hunting, you can contact JAN, a free telephone counseling service that will enable you to figure out how to work with your disability to reach your goals.

The Job Accommodation Network is funded by the governments of the United States and Canada. It is headquartered at West Virginia University.

If you call JAN, you will be put in touch with a specialized counselor who has access to over 250,000 successful accommodations in a computerized database. Manufacturers write them about their newest equipment. And the people at JAN spend all day talking to people solving employment-related problems.

Anyone can call them: job-hunters with disabilities, employers, counselors, doctors -- even relatives of job-hunters. You might tell them, for example,

"I want to be hired as a _____, and I found a prospective employer. They told me I had to _____ as part of the job, and I don't think I can do that. I acted like I could and I need to show them how I'll do it. Is there any gadget or tool or any strategy that will solve this problem for us? The JAN counselor (they call them "human factor consultants") will ask you to describe:

- The nature of your disability, and what it limits you in being able to do.
- The job, and what tasks it requires you to perform.
- What equipment you have to perform the job.

some interesting politics -- or believe there might be a problem where you could assist. In other words, you are sensing things that are not written down.

So, you need to go talk to someone. When you do, you get some questions answered, but they also recommend some things you might read. Now, you read for awhile, and then you have more questions. Written research, oral research, written research, oral research, and so on.

- What problem task remains, that is, what task you are asking JAN to help you figure out some way to do - - or some way to get around.

JAN will search their database and formulate strategies for dealing with the problem. Within twenty-four hours (usually) they will call you back or send you a summary that suggests devices, procedures, or other ways of dealing with the problem. They will also send you information about the manufacturers of any devices they may suggest, and in some cases, they may refer you to employers who have successfully dealt with this problem.

JAN counselors will help you with other aspects of your job search such as handling an application that is difficult to fill out because of your disability, preemployment testing challenges, and handling ADA issues, such as illegal interview questions. And, of course, they will help you with problems at your current job.

JAN Contact Information:

Job Accommodation Network
West Virginia University
P.O. Box 6080
Morgantown, WV 26506–6080

Phone: Toll free 800-526-7234 (Voice/TTY)
ADA Information: 800-232-9675 (Voice/TTY)
Fax: 304-293-5407
Web site: http://janweb.icdi.wvu.edu

Most people have a preference for either written research or oral research - - and you should lean toward the mode that you find the most effective. On the other hand, if you avoid one mode altogether, you will miss too much information. Accommodate your disability as you work this process. If you generally do poorly in face-to-face contacts, make sure that you are extremely knowledgeable through your reading before you approach someone. And if your blindness means that you read very slowly, but you are great at remembering what you hear--and people generally like you--well, then do as much research as possible using the telephone and visits to people. You probably already do this instinctively.

As you read the following section, you may find some technology is mentioned that is not familiar to you. In that case, call the Job Accommodation Network or your state technology center, which was funded by the "Tech Act" (see page 137). Now, we want to present some specific disability-related problems that might come up as you do research along with some solutions to those problems.

Research Using Written Sources. A good way to start figuring out where you want to work is usually by studying journals, books, and other documents as well as Web sites.

▶ **Challenge:**
You have difficulty reading due to blindness, dyslexia, or another impairment.

▶ **Responses:**
1. Get information from e-mail, the Internet, or computer databases. Use voice recognition technology.
2. Use a reading machine that will scan the material and then read it back to you in a human-sounding voice.
3. Use Braille, if you know how.
4. Find CD-ROM or disk versions of the material and use them.

▶ **Challenge:**
You have difficulty reading small print, which many directories use.

▶ **Responses:**
1. Find the CD-ROM version and use it in a computer. Many computers have software that magnifies print. And you

Resources for Recorded Materials

The National Library Service for the Blind and Physically Handicapped, The Library of Congress, Washington, DC 20542 has put many books on career planning and job-hunting on tape. If you have a disability that prevents you from reading standard printed material, they will send the tapes to your home with special playback equipment and free return postage. The disability must be medically documented. Go to your local library and ask for information on your regional library service for the blind and physically handicapped.

Recording for the Blind & Dyslexic, 20 Roszel Road, Princeton, NJ 08540 (phone: 800-221-4792) has also recorded job-hunting books for people with visual impairments and dyslexia. You must be registered to use the service.

can buy software packages to enable your computer to magnify print if your current operating system can't do it.
2. Use a magnifying glass.
3. If you are copying, go slowly and put an index card under the place you want to copy.
4. Use equipment, such as CCTV (Closed-Circuit Television), that magnifies print.

▶ **Challenge:**
You read well, but have not been taught how to conduct research or feel intimidated by it. This often happens to people with disabilities who have inadequate education. First, you notice that you can't get started. Then you use willpower. You conscientiously try to do research, but still can't seem to find the facts you need.

▶ **Responses:**
1. Determine exactly what you want to learn and then ask a librarian how to find it. Librarians are often extremely

helpful. Go at a time when the library is least crowded, which is usually 10 A.M. to 11 A.M. and 2 P.M. to 4 P.M. on weekdays.

2. Take classes on how to do research. Some libraries offer free orientations. Try your community colleges, adult education offerings, and other trainings. Internet research classes are sometimes offered through computer stores.

3. Hire a "research mentor." You might ask a graduate student to assist you.

Research Involving Talking to People. Conduct informational interviews in person or by telephone. Ask what people like or dislike about their jobs. Find out about trends. They might indicate needs you can uniquely fill. Ask people if X organization can use your skills. Explain your rationale and see if they agree. Then, if they do, ask who you can talk to at that organization. Informational interviews may also be used to find out details about the person who has the power to hire you -- as well as how to get to see them.

If you ask people about things that tap their unique knowledge, you will probably find they are glad to talk to you. Avoid asking them about information that is easily available from written sources. This might make them think that you are not serious about your job search and they may not want to refer you to those people whom they truly respect. You need do your homework -- and not waste their time.

When you seek and set up an informational interview, remember that **you** are in charge of requesting it, scheduling it, and structuring it. But, **nobody owes you an informational interview**. In addition, you are responsible for your own accommodation, if you need one for your disability.

Here are some challenges that come up for people with disabilities, followed by useful responses:

▶ **Challenge:**

You have difficulty conducting conversations due to deafness, being hard of hearing, having a speech impediment, or any number of disabilities.

▶ **Responses:**

1. Arrange an interview using e-mail, either writing to the person being interviewed or "talking" online.

2. Deaf or hard-of-hearing people might want to use the telephone relay service. Trouble is, the telephone relay service is time consuming and difficult for hearing people. Our recommendation is to avoid use of the telephone unless the person you are calling has access to a text telephone (TTY). You might set up an online "chat" if you and the person have the same online service provider or ones that are compatible. Or you might consider paying for an interpreter to help you with your informational interviews. For a less expensive alternative, try asking an interpreter training school if a student trainee could do the interpreting.

3. If you have a speech impediment that is serious, bring a friend, a personal assistant, or a professional interpreter (not a parent or counselor) to repeat what you say.

4. Consider technological solutions such as the Liberator, a computerized keyboard with artificial speech capabilities. You press the keys and it talks for you.

▶ **Challenge:**

You can talk, but have difficulty with language. You talk slowly or there are long pauses in the conversation.

▶ **Responses:**

1. Memorize and practice "scripts," which might include the questions you plan to ask, a thirty-second snapshot of your skills, or a description of the type of organization you

are seeking. If you use artificial speech, program your statements in advance.

2. If anything about your speech annoys people or gives the wrong impression, say something about it to put the person at ease. You might say, "Some people find that I talk slowly. Please be patient with me."

3. Bring a pad and paper along in case you get stuck.

4. If the person who you've been talking with has been gracious and patient with you, thank them. If they are less than patient, keep calm. **Be patient with other people's impatience with you**. Repeat your statement slowly and rephrase, if necessary. End the interview if you sense the person is overwhelmed, angry, or has stopped paying attention.

▶ Challenge:

You are afraid to actually call someone up and ask for an interview.

▶ Responses:

1. Remember that's a fear that you share with everyone. It's probably worse for you, because you have had more bad experiences with meeting people you don't know. However, for some people the best solution is to recognize that it is normal to feel that way. Sometimes one simply has to choose the path of courage. So, just do it.

2. Practice informational interviews with people you already know who make you feel comfortable. Sometimes it is helpful to write down all of the things you fear that someone will say -- then have your friend say them -- and you practice responses.

3. Career counselors and vocational counselors can help you overcome this fear. They use techniques such as having you think through and evaluate the source of your fear or practicing with you until you are confident.

▶ **Challenge:**

You have difficulty understanding what you are told and particularly have difficulty taking notes and remembering the facts later.

▶ **Responses:**

1. Repeat back what the person says to be sure you understand.
2. You may be tempted to ask if you can tape-record the session. Be careful, though. This can make the person feel defensive and less willing to talk freely. We recommend against it in most cases.
3. Write down your best recollection of the informational interview immediately afterward. You might want to locate a coffee shop or a bench where you will go as soon as you complete the interview.

Step 3: How Do You Obtain Such a Job?

Find the person who has the power to hire you. Make a presentation to that person about how your skills meet their needs. Persuade them to give you a fair salary for your skills.

At this point, your disability should not be a strong factor. However, your strategy for approaching this person should include how you will handle their reactions to your disability. Here are some ideas:

▶ **Challenge:**

People often do not get a good first impression of you. This may be because of some aspect of your visible disability that causes prejudice, or how you talk or move, or difficulties in getting along with others, due to lack of social contact and experience.

▶ **Responses:**

1. Do everything you can to make a good first impression. Get rid of the small things that you can control. Be freshly

bathed, use deodorant, and have your fingernails neatly cut, for example. If you are male, have your face freshly shaved or your hair and beard freshly trimmed. If you are female, have your hair newly styled. *What Color Is Your Parachute?* and other books on job interviews cover this thoroughly.

2. Before visiting the person who has the power to hire you, find ways to create a halo effect--to make them eager to meet you and to overlook the factors that have bothered other people. For example, you might have some mutual friends call them and make positive comments about you in an informal manner. You might write a letter outlining your ideas. You might start a relationship with them by telephone and e-mail. Then, you will already be friends when the face-to-face meeting begins.

▶ Challenge:

Your network contacts have told you that this person is seeing you only because they feel sorry for you--as their "good deed for the day."

▶ Response:

Congratulations on knowing this ahead of time! It shows that you are doing the process right--you have people who are rooting for you and who are willing to tell you the truth. The trick here is to forget about that possibility when you meet the person. Ask questions and listen well to their responses. Develop rapport. And enthusiastically explain how you can help solve their problems (that is, the ones **they** think they have, not the one **you** think they have). They won't feel sorry for you for long. Their pity **will** turn into respect.

▶ Challenge:

When people meet you, they sometimes find your disability so shocking they can't stop noticing your disability--and won't start focusing on you.

▶ **Response:**

If you have a visible, obvious disability, such as using a wheelchair, cerebral palsy, blindness, or Down's syndrome, consider telling them ahead of time. Do it calmly and without fanfare. For example, "Thank you for having such an accessible building, I use a wheelchair," or "I am blind, so don't be surprised by my cane." Remember, if you did your research well and found a person with a problem that you are likely to solve -- and have seen to it that they know good things about you before you come -- they may be as eager to meet you as you are to meet them.

CREATIVE JOB-HUNTING: AN EXCELLENT STRATEGY FOR PEOPLE WITH DISABILITIES

Despite the challenges just discussed, the creative job-hunting technique works far better than the numbers game for people with disabilities, not only because of its "track record" that shows it works for 86 percent of the folks who try it, but also because:

- The entire process of studying and selling your strengths **contradicts** any negative attitudes about yourself you may have picked up from others. You will become specific about what you *can* do. Most people with disabilities have been told over and over and over again what they *can't* do. As you work through this process, you will leave all of the "can'ts" behind.

- As you meet people for informational interviews, since these are just interviews for information, when the time is right, you can frankly discuss any aspect of your disability that concerns you. Anyone who agrees to meet you for an informational interview has no agenda to screen you out. It is a meeting between equals.

- If your disability causes a great deal of discrimination or if you have challenging accommodation needs, you need to be particularly careful about finding a job that you will do excellently. Through the creative job-hunting process, you can tell people about the contributions you have to offer. Your thorough research is likely to earn their respect. This makes it easier to figure out which employers are most likely to be willing to overlook the problems you present so they can obtain the contributions you can offer to their firm.

- You can find out **details** about the tasks required for each job. And before you are interviewed by someone who has the power to hire (or not hire) you for the job, you can find out which tasks need to be modified for your disability and figure out how that could be done.

- You don't have to limit yourself to searching for a traditional job or those jobs that are available. Suppose you have a special need. For example, suppose you need three half-days a week off during business hours for a particular therapy in order to keep healthy and alive. (Eighty-five percent of people with disabilities[2] who are not employed say their disability or health problem severely limits what they can do.) How many advertised jobs are going to conform to your schedule? But if you have assessed your strengths -- and can describe them -- you can search for an employer who needs your talents enough that they will let you work on the schedule **you** require.

- You can find out about **the organizational "culture"** of the places you are considering for employment. So, for example, if you find out that such and such a corporation is well known for its family friendly policies and that schedules are frequently changed for parents of young children,

---

2. *1998 N.O.D./Harris Survey of Americans with Disabilities*, 46.

you can consider it more seriously as a place to work. Such a place is very likely to make changes that you need as well. On the other hand, if you discover the CEO of company X thinks diversity is a bunch of poppycock--and that there are no women in their management group, and that the company has hired only three people with minority backgrounds and two were fired a year later, well, then you might avoid that company.

- If you find out that X company is innovative, has great management practices, and works hard to keep its employees, you could logically assume they would be flexible with you as well. But, if you find out that this is a rule-based bureaucratic company that insists everyone do everything in the same way, and your accommodation needs require that things be done in a slightly different way, you may want to avoid that company.

- Since there is no particular job at stake, a future employer will often take in your strengths--and keep you in mind for needs that come up. Your disability stops being an issue. This contrasts with what happens when you interview for a vacant position. The interviewer measures you against an ideal person they imagine will fit an opening. They might think about the ADA and feel constrained by legal issues. With a less formal process, if the person with the power to hire you likes you, they can think about every need and challenge they have--and think about possibilities for you working somewhere in the company.

- You are active rather than passive. You don't sit around and wait for people to call you--you call people and ask for their assistance. You not only help yourself, but if you are a well-prepared informational interviewer, you may change your contact's attitudes toward all people with disabilities.

The creative job-hunting process works for 86 percent of people who try it. It is particularly helpful for people with disabilities. And as we saw earlier, the numbers game, unfortunately, is particularly unhelpful.

RULES ABOUT COMPETING FOR OPENINGS

Despite the problems caused by the numbers game, the creative job-hunting process is not for everyone. If you have real difficulties in one-on-one discussions with others, creative job-hunting may not work. Creative job-hunting requires imagination, boldness, and the ability to communicate your skills to others. And, the creative job-hunting process might uncover an opening--one that is a perfect fit. In that case, you would have to apply and compete for the position.

Remember, the numbers game of getting resumes and cover letters out to as many employers as possible works for some people. Using the Internet and posting a resume has a 1 percent success rate for people who are looking for nontechnical jobs. Mailing resumes out to employers at random and answering ads in newspapers has a 7 percent success rate. That is, seven out of every one hundred job seekers who use this method find a job that way. Answering local newspaper ads has a 5 to 24 percent success rate.

The low success rate of the numbers game does **not** mean that it is the wrong strategy for you. It can be easier to impress an employer who has a good impression of you from reading a well-crafted resume and cover letter. It is helpful that they want to hire *somebody* for the position.

With a lot of effort, you may be able to beat the low odds. To compete successfully, you will need skills that are in demand, learn how to present them powerfully on paper, and learn to give the best possible interview.

You might also ask for job leads from family members, friends, and people in the community (33 percent success rate); or use the phone book's Yellow Pages to call employers and ask if they are hiring for the position that you want (69 percent success rate).

However, looking for work when you do **not** create a job is essentially a matter of finding out about a job and **competing** for it. That is true for anybody. If you are a person who happens to have a disability, what is different is that you face tougher competition. The rules that apply to all job-hunters, therefore, apply to you in double measure. You *must* arm yourself the best you can for the competition you will face. There are hurdles and obstacles that you must overcome, both "out there" and inside yourself.

The main obstacles "out there" are, of course, the ignorance, fear, anxiety, prejudice, and discrimination that you will run into with employers or your future coworkers. Much of this is based on ignorance, which *you* will have to dispel yourself. As a **job-hunter with a disability, part of your task in job-hunting is that you will often have to educate would-be employers as you go.**

And one thing you will need to do as you educate them is deal with their fears--which is what the next chapter will cover.

CHAPTER 4

The Fears an Employer Has When Interviewing People with Disabilities

AND HOW YOU CAN PERSUADE THEM THAT YOU ARE QUALIFIED

Whether you use the "numbers game" or the "creative job-hunting" approach, you will be meeting employers. And when you find employers that interest you, you will need to approach them. You will need to talk to them face to face, because employers never hire a stranger. The main thing to remember with *any* employer is that **every employer has fears**, and that much of your task during the job interview is to try to put these fears to rest. You, of course, want to know what *particular* fears the employer is likely to entertain because you have a disability. So let's open that Pandora's box.

EMPLOYER FEARS: WHAT THEY ARE AND HOW TO HANDLE THEM

If you could read an employer's thoughts as they conduct a job interview with a person with a disability, this is what you might hear:

> **"I don't exactly understand what this person's disability is, and I'm afraid to ask."**

This has always been a fear for employers - - and the ADA has made the fear worse, since it forbids employers to ask about the disability (because in the past, these questions were used to screen out people with disabilities). So the employer not only has the uneasiness, prejudice, discrimination, or whatever we want to call it, but they are also sometimes afraid of being sued.

You must figure out how to disarm this fear. You will not help matters if you merely stand and deliver the title of your disability. The employer may still be as mystified as before, and *still* afraid to ask. Instead, before you even go into any kind of job-seeking interview (or *any* of the types of interviews mentioned in this book), memorize the answers to these questions:

1. What is it that I can do and do well?
2. What are my limitations? What is it that I can't do or find extremely difficult to do?
3. What can I tell them about the ways and strategies I have developed for getting around these limitations? For example, be prepared to describe the computer software you use in order to have the computer "talk" to you or to enlarge the print you need to read.
4. What is it that I have learned *through* my disability? For example, you have learned excellent time-management skills because you must work around treatment needs that take one-and-a-half hours a day.

Then when you are face to face with an employer, simply find an opportune time in the interview to recite these four things, in exactly that order, and this should put that fear to rest, forever. Next fear?

"Will my insurance go up if I hire this person?"

You have to figure out how to disarm this fear. This is probably the most common fear among employers, and there is no basis for it. In a recent survey of human resource executives from over eight hundred companies, 81 percent said that they had **not** had an insurer decline, limit, or exclude health, life, and/or long-term disability coverage to employees or dependents with disabilities.[1] You may also want to bring up the tax benefits discussed on page 70. Next fear?

"I want to hire this person, but what if there is some problem adapting this particular job to their limitations, and neither they nor I know how to solve this problem?"

You have to figure out how to disarm this fear. Fortunately, if you followed all of the steps of creative job-hunting--and did thorough research *before* you met the person with the power to hire you--disarming this fear should be *easy.* You already know what is probably required; all you have to do is to explain how you will handle it. You may even impress the employer as someone who has done their homework--something that is still not as common as employers would like. Of course, you should get as much detail as possible from the actual employer during the interview before you say anything. Thus you might say, "This is a picture of my Visualtek. It's what I need to read documents--I can bring it with me." Or, "I have only one hand, but I am a whiz at the computer. Almost all software can adapt to this one-handed typing keyboard, which I learned to use in rehab. True, I don't type as fast as others, but I think before I write, so I do fewer drafts. And you won't lose any time when you want urgent reports from me." Next fear?

---

1. *The ADA at Work: Implementation of the Employment Provisions of the Americans with Disabilities Act,* prepared by the Society for Human Resource Management, Cornell University School of Industrial and Labor Relations; The Lewin Group, and Washington Business Group on Health (Alexandria, VA: 1999), 9.

"How much will it cost me to hire this person? If they need extra accommodations, it may cost my entire budget."

You have to figure out how to disarm this fear. Just figure out the least costly way for them to accommodate you and tell them about it. Be specific. You might tell them, for example, about Sticky Keys -- the software on many computer programs that allows you to press one key, for example, the shift key, and then the computer holds the key down while you hit another. You get the same effect from the computer that you would have if you had held the first key down yourself with your own finger. So your problem in using your hand won't matter. If possible, we recommend that you offer to buy whatever aids you need, or arrange to have them with you. Check with Vocational Rehabilitation and your state Tech Act Project for Assistive Technology Devices and Services (described in resources section of this book). If not, your employer might agree to buy it.

If it is true (and it often is), the easiest way to allay the fear of the costs of hiring you is to point out to the employer that there are no costs. In fact, 20 percent of the accommodations surveyed by the Job Accommodation Network cost nothing; 51 percent cost between $1 and $500; and 11 percent cost between $501 and $1,000.[2] You can also let your employer know about the Job Accommodation Network (800-526-7234), a resource that is publicly funded and available to both of you if problems come up (see page 52).

If there is a cost, you must explain it, offer options, and make it clear that **the costs will not exceed a certain limit.**

---

2. President's Committee on Employment of People with Disabilities' Job Accommodation Network, *Accommodation Benefit/Cost Data* --Tabulated through July 30, 1999, page 4. (Morgantown, WV: President's Committee on Employment of People with Disabilities/Job Accommodation Network, 1999).

If your accommodation needs appear costly to the employer, tell them about the **tax incentives** for making accommodation. That is, any employer may deduct up to $15,000 each year to remove a barrier for people who are elderly or disabled.[3] A variety of expenses can be included, such as interpreters for people who are deaf, readers for people who are blind, or special equipment such as a reading machine or removing architectural barriers, such as making a bathroom usable for you.[4]

If you are considering working at a small business (defined by the IRS as one having thirty or fewer full-time employees or one earning less than one million dollars a year), tell them about the Disabled Access Credit (IRS Code 44).[5] The business receives a credit of 50 percent of expenditures between $250 and $10,250 for accommodation, up to a maximum benefit of $5,000. This amount is subtracted from their taxes -- so they end up basically only paying half price for the accommodation (unless, of course, they are paying almost no taxes).

You also might want to explain how accommodating workers with disabilities often adds to innovation and productivity for all. Ramps, put in for people in wheelchairs, are preferred by most people over steps -- and cut down on falls and accidents. The Jacuzzi was invented by a man whose son had an illness that required hot baths. And captioned TV, which started as a way hearing-impaired people could watch television, is now used in health clubs and bars and other noisy places for everyone to enjoy TV shows. If you have a story that relates to your own disability, use it. Next fear?

---

3. *Business Expenses for Use in Preparing 1999 Tax Returns* (Publication 535), Department of the Treasury, IRS, 38–40. Order from the IRS at 800-829-3676 (voice), 800-829-4059 (TTY), or www.irs.gov.

4. Form 8826, Department of the Treasury, IRS. Order from the IRS (see above).

5. *Tax Incentives for Business*, President's Committee on Employment of People with Disabilities (Washington, DC, 1997).

"I know this job-hunter may be able to do this job as it is structured now, but things are changing faster than I can keep track of . . . and what if something else comes along that I haven't thought of--and we can't come up with a way to get around their disability at that point?"

You have to figure out how to disarm this fear. First, if there was a time when you figured out on your own how to get around your disability so you could do an important task, tell that story. You could then add, "Could you please give me some idea of how you have designed this job in your organization? I feel quite confident that I could do the job in general. As for the particular tasks that might give me a problem, as I've demonstrated, I'm usually able to figure out a way to get them accomplished." This is another situation where you might want to tell the employer about the Job Accommodation Network or that you have friends with similar difficulties who would help you brainstorm ideas if you have problems. The key is to be clear that **you** will take the responsibility for handling your disability--and that you will be proactive in getting around it so as to *do the job.* Next fear?

"Just exactly how would this person get to work?"

You have to figure out how to disarm this fear. Of course you wouldn't be applying for the job if you didn't know how to get there. So just explain that to the employer. You might say, "I can't drive, so I take the bus. The X-5 is fairly reliable in the morning. And I always catch the bus ahead of the one I would absolutely have to take. That way, I will definitely be here on time, or even ahead of time, even if the bus service is unreliable on a particular day." Or "A lot of people think there is a transportation problem for people who use wheelchairs. Well, I have a van with a lift that brings my wheelchair to the driver's seat. I notice that you have parking for people with disabilities. My van is very, very reliable. And my wheelchair fits in my husband's car--he can take me if by chance my van breaks down." Go into detail, in this manner. It will demonstrate to the employer that you've thought of everything. Next fear?

"What if I hire this disabled person, and they don't work out? What if they quit? What if I have to fire them? I'll be accused of firing them because they are disabled, with maybe a lawsuit in the offing. I can't take that kind of heat."

You have to figure out how to disarm this fear. People with disabilities are not any more likely to need firing than anyone else. In a survey of managers by Lou Harris and Associates, 24 percent of top managers (*in companies that had hired employees with disabilities*) rated their employees' job performance as excellent; 64 percent rated it as good. Only 5 percent called it fair and 1 percent called it poor.[6]

The fact that people with disabilities don't have some perverse need to be fired may be obvious to you, but what should you say to the employer? Try words such as these: "My injury (or disability) has been a blessing in disguise, because it's forced me to choose a career that I can do well and stay in permanently. If you're willing to take a chance on me, I'll give it my very best shot. But, if things don't work out to our mutual satisfaction, I'd want you to tell me that straight out, and I'll pick up my tent peaceably, and move on." Next fear?

---

6. *The ICD* [International Center for the Disabled] *Survey II: Employing Disabled Americans,* conducted by Louis Harris and Associates, Inc., in cooperation with the National Council on the Handicapped and the President's Committee on Employment of the Handicapped (New York: Louis Harris and Associates, 1987), 7. Note: There is no more recent Harris Poll of managers.

**"How is this person with a disability going to
get along with the other workers? What if my
other employees are jealous of this new employee
because they do a superb job, and the other
employees feel that casts some aspersions on
them? What if I have to promote them over the
heads of other workers, on merit alone? I'm afraid
that those who were passed over might attribute
the promotion solely to my feeling sorry about
this person's disability, rather than to their ability;
and, if they're angry about it, may bring dissen-
sion into my workplace."**

This is a well-grounded fear, *and you must figure out how to
address it.* The problem of myths and stereotypes covers the
whole population -- unfortunately including the people you
will be working with if hired. And many people with disabilities, like most minority groups, *overcompensate*, that is, work
harder than most people to make up for their disability, a
strategy that can indeed lead to jealousy from coworkers. You
may want to defuse this fear before it is brought up. You could
tell a story about how your ability to get along well with
your coworkers was helpful in your last job -- or your ability
to work with your fellow students assisted the school you attended. Or, you could say, "Wherever I work, I tend to develop
a natural rapport with my fellow workers, so that they're
rooting for **me** as much as I'm rooting for **them.**" Next fear?

**"How is this person with a disability going to
communicate with others at work? I'm afraid
that's going to be a serious difficulty."**

You have to figure out how to disarm this fear. You need to
show absolutely excellent communication skills during the
interview and be ready to explain communication problems
and solutions. For example, if you are a person who is deaf,

you might say, "In the past, it hasn't been a problem. With friends and fellow workers, I sometimes lip-read, I sometimes write, and I also teach some simple sign language to them. It always worked out just fine." Next fear?

"How will this person who has a disability avoid accidents on the job? I'm afraid they will be a safety hazard."

You have to figure out how to disarm this fear. It's a big one. Volunteering your own past safety record is one way to put this fear to rest. You might tell them how your disability has made you more careful than before--and that you are a stickler for all safety rules. You might even tell them how you will help contribute to better safety among all employees. For example, if you are a person with a back injury who has learned proper lifting techniques (the hard way, unfortunately), you can point out to the employer that you would be able to offer informal "inservice training" to the other employees about how to lift objects safely. Next fear?

"What if this person with a history of mental illness gets violent? What will I do if they lose their temper, or even pick fights with other employees?"

This fear actually applies to other disabilities as well. For example, people with attention deficit disorder are thought to be "impulsive." This fear prevents many people with disabilities from being hired. *You must address this fear*. The best way is to tell a detailed story about a highly stressful situation that you handled well. "When I was a customer service agent at the airport, I was nearly attacked by a passenger who thought that it was my fault his flight was delayed. Fortunately, I know how to handle stress--my own and others. I took several deep breaths, listened to him calmly, and let him wind down, then called my supervisor so we could work on his problem." And now on to the last fear.

"How will this person with a disability handle emergencies, such as a fire in the building? I'm afraid they could get burned or killed, and I don't want responsibility for that on my shoulders."

You have to figure out how to disarm this fear. If you use a wheelchair, you might want to tell them there are many options to get you out in case of fire--and describe how you have handled the problem in the past, (i.e., the fire department designating a spot where you wait for rescue, a specialized chair that can be used to carry you, and so on). If you are deaf, you might let them know where to purchase lights for their alarm system--and let them know that this improves the safety for all, as the warning lights help attract everyone's attention. If you are blind, inform them that you can easily leave the building in case of emergency. And again, you can always call the Job Accommodation Network staff and ask for their thoughts, if you honestly have no idea how you would get out of that particular building.

Well, there you have it: the major fears employers have about hiring someone with a disability. Whatever words you come up with to lay these fears to rest, be sure to use language that feels *natural* to you. Brainstorming with your family, or friends, or counselor about this should help. If you are able to quiet the employer's fears, get them to like you, and have the right qualifications, you are very likely to get the job.

PERSUADING EMPLOYERS THAT YOU ARE QUALIFIED

In order to get hired, you **must** convince them that you are qualified. Just because somebody turns you down for a job does **not** necessarily mean they are discriminating against you. Your experience, education, and abilities just might not match the particular set of tasks they need to get done.

But first, remember the two types of employers we discussed earlier:

- Those who are bothered by your disability and will discriminate actively or passively; and

- Those who are not bothered and will give you a chance-- or those who are a little bothered, but are enlightened enough to notice their own feelings and overcome them to the extent they are able. They are willing to treat you fairly.

If you are unable to persuade the employers you meet to overcome their fears, you are probably meeting with too many who are in the first group.

But here is the key: When it comes to the second group, you **must** persuade them that you are qualified--that you are the one in two hundred employees who can truly help them do what **they** need to get done.

Convincing them that you can meet their needs is *your* job during the interview. **If you are somehow failing to do this then that failure--not your disability--is causing you to get turned down.**

If you know you are qualified, and simply can't convince them, consider offering to work on a short assignment as a consultant. Another idea is to *volunteer* your services, without pay, for a set period of time at that place (two weeks to two months). If they tell you there is a legal problem, offer to serve as an intern. *If* they take you up on that offer (they may not), this gives the employer a chance to look at your work *without any risk or cost.* There is *no* guarantee that this will eventually get you a job there, but it is a strategy that *has* paid off many times for job-hunters. So it's certainly worth a shot, *if you can afford to do it.*

Volunteering may also be a winning strategy for you if you
need to gain **experience** in the job market when you don't
have any. A little over half of human resource managers surveyed (51 percent) said that lack of related experience was a
major barrier to them hiring people with disabilities in their
company.[7] In this case, you should volunteer for some internship or other on-the-job training program. Volunteering at a
place that truly interests you is also an attractive option if you
are dying to work, but with your present benefit package you
cannot really *afford* to take a job, lest you lose those benefits
and medical coverage. By volunteering your services, you get
a chance to keep your benefits, and still use your God-given
talents or abilities, toward making this world a better place.

Whether you volunteer, give an excellent interview, or use
the creative job-hunting process, the reality is that you **must
convince a person who has the power to hire you that
you are the right employee for the job**.

Facing up to this reality shows a lot of guts. You are saying,
**"I am responsible. I am willing to examine what I am
doing and change it."** You are not giving into the too-easy
path of victimhood--a major temptation in our society,
which routinely encourages people to blame factors outside
their control: their dysfunctional families, their employers,
society, and, of course, their disability.

You may be having problems persuading employers to
hire you because you are applying for jobs that are too difficult. You may simply be aiming *too high*. There are two common reasons for this among people with disabilities. One is
that you were at a certain level before your injury or illness
and you naturally expect to go back to the way you were.
But, in certain cases, such as brain injury or chronic fatigue
syndrome or other illnesses, *this won't happen*.

---

7. *The ADA at Work*, 5.

You must be realistic about what you can do. If the accident impaired your intelligence, you may never again be able to supervise hundreds of people. If your chronic fatigue is severe, you may not be able to work full-time.

A second possible reason is a history of receiving overly positive feedback about yourself. Another possibility: You were lazy when you assessed your strengths . . . and just wrote down the strengths you wished you had, but didn't bother to check them against reality. This is why it is critical to be **thorough** in your self-assessment at the beginning of your job-hunt. That way, you don't waste your time or the employer's time attempting to obtain a job that you can't do well anyway.

But, if your aim is right and you still aren't getting job offers, you must change the situation and get job offers. And the key is recognizing that you might be at fault, that you might be doing something wrong or inappropriate - - in short, you might be sabotaging yourself. Your experience as a person with a disability might have caused you to learn the wrong lessons - - lessons that get in the way of effectively persuading employers to hire you. The next chapter discusses how to unlearn these wrong lessons, overcome your own fears, and get hired.

CHAPTER 5

Overcoming Your Own Fears

AND AVOIDING SELF-SABOTAGE

Most job-hunters think that after one interview, the employer decides if they will hire you. Not true. For most jobs, you will experience a series of interviews. After the first, the second, and even the third interview, you must continue to work on getting the job and continue to address any fears that you think were not handled effectively in the discussion. You must continue to do this until you get the job.

You can use follow-up letters and e-mails. You can ask your contacts to put in a good word for you. They can help you address an employer's fears, particularly if your potential boss thinks you can't do the job because of your disability or might have trouble fitting in. References can vouch for your past accomplishments, your resourcefulness, and your good nature.

You might have to do *many* interviews in order to locate a job opening. You might do lots of research. You might visit many people who have the power to hire you. Then you find out, after all this, that you can't *really* solve their problem. Or that you would have been great -- but couldn't convince them of that fact.

And this may happen again and again.

To get a job, you might have to do this fifty or sixty different times. Giving up after just six interviews and six turn-downs is tossing in the towel *much too soon.*

Now, why toss in the towel at that point? After all, you have the momentum from the preparation for those six interviews. And succeeding in getting an interview, however you did it, is an achievement in itself.

There are several reasons why people toss the towel in too early. One is that most people (with or without disabilities) **completely underestimate the difficulty and time involved in job-hunting.** They honestly think that they are supposed to get a job in one week. Not true.

The second reason is the rejection shock we discussed earlier. Most of us hate being rejected. And after being rejected six times, there is a natural, human tendency to want to lick our wounds and hide away -- which will **definitely not** result in an employer coming after you to offer you the magic job.

The third problem has to do with your own fears and with the way that you see yourself as a person with a disability.

INTERNAL AND EXTERNAL OPPRESSION

It is helpful to notice, in all of this, that there are two kinds of oppression: **external oppression** and **internal oppression.** External oppression refers to the **real** barriers, **real** prejudices, and **real** problems we face as people with disabilities.

Internal oppression refers to the way we can start thinking about ourselves. We think we **deserve** these problems, that we are less than others, that we can't work, that we can't continue the process of job-hunting, or that we should be **grateful** to anyone who even **thinks of hiring** us.

For example, let us say you are a college student and you have cerebral palsy. And you want to be a doctor. So, you start talking to your pre-med advisor and he says, "Look, don't try to be a doctor. It's too difficult with your condition, you won't be able to make it through the internship, and medical schools won't accept you. Why don't you think about a less demanding profession?"

That experience is an example of **external** oppression. It becomes **internal** oppression if you become depressed, start thinking this advisor is right, and don't bother to do the research that might prove him wrong. If you do research, you might call the American Medical Association and the American Medical Student Association and say, "Hey, I was just told there was no such thing as a doctor who has cerebral palsy. I find that a little hard to believe. Do you know anyone who might know a doctor who has cerebral palsy, or who has some kind of disability?" You could get on the Internet and start posting inquiries on every related bulletin board you could find. And if you can't find such a person, you could then start asking the next question, "OK, how can I be the first doctor who happens to have cerebral palsy?"

Another example: You are injured and you are in rehabilitation in the hospital. In order to get your medical care paid for and your salary continued through long-term disability, you have to go through a lot of paperwork and get doctors' notes saying that you are not able to work. To get the income support, the insurance rules of Social Security and some private companies insist that you **prove** that you are not able to work at all!

This system is an example of **external** oppression. If you and your doctor were to tell the truth -- which is that you are not presently working, but you have **every intention** of figuring out how you can contribute again and that you are **sure** it is possible -- well, assistance might be withheld and you and your family just might starve and you might not get the medical care you need. Then you definitely would become one of the people who cannot escape the clutches of this system that pays you to be idle and will not let you work.

The **internal** oppression starts when you believe those forms you fill out and when you truly believe that "disabled" means unable to work. By the way, the system is very convincing--and only an elite few make it back to work. This is because what you do affects what you think. In this case, you have to prove that you can't work. You explain why you can't work, get doctors to document that you can't work, and follow the advice of your lawyer to show that you can't work. So, if you are like most people, you begin to believe that you can't work.

But, the truth is **that there is a job that you can do and a contribution you can make**. And your goal should be to overcome the internal oppression--and **find** the job you can do.

You know the bad news: It is true that there may be nothing immediate you can do about the external oppression. Now, here is the good news: You have complete power over whether or not you accept the internal oppression. You decide what you think--and you can act against the internal oppression. **You can become a shining light**--a person who proves everyone else wrong.

Overcoming internal oppression means **disbelieving the damaging myths** that "the world" out there believes and uses to justify not hiring us.

And what are those myths? Their nature is evident if you just examine *the dark thoughts* that those of us with disabilities often have when we first set out job-hunting. We compare ourselves, of course, with those who don't have any disabilities. We think negative thoughts and hear them in our head. They come out something like this:

I *am disabled*, they are not; I *am filled with a sense of what I cannot do*, while they are filled with a sense of what they can do; I *am set apart from the rest of humankind*, they are not; I *have nothing in common with an employer*, while they do; I *have to ask the employer to redesign the job to accommodate my limitations*, while they do not.

82

All of these thoughts are common, but *all of these thoughts are untrue*. Treating them as though they were true will inevitably cause the hopelessness you were trying to avoid.

It is a particularly difficult problem when you have been rejected many times. You, of course, want to blame it on something. *Who doesn't?* The first tempting target, when you have a disability, is to think *your disability* is the reason you are being turned down. And that may be the case. In this world we live in, it **is** harder to find a job if you have a disability--and you will have to do even more interviews and letters and phone calls and work than people who do not have disabilities.

But there is another possibility that you must face. And that is that your disability is **not** the reason you are being turned down. The reality is that you might be presenting yourself poorly. You might be inadvertently convincing the employer that you **should** be screened out. Or that you are not the one in two hundred applicants that can help solve the organization's problems. In short, you might be botching up your interviews.

EXAMPLES OF BOTCHED-UP INTERVIEWS

Well, OK, **how** might you be botching up these interviews with employers? And **why** might you be botching them up? Well, *simple inexperience* in this business of interviewing for a job (or for information leading to a job) is one very obvious reason. Also, you may have no desire at all to go back to work (if you became disabled, for example, at a job you hated)-- but you need to go through *the appearances* of job-hunting, in order to mollify your friends, family, or counselors who may be working very hard to support you, with the expectation that *this support is temporary*.

These are the kinds of reasons we may be conscious of. And then there is the vast realm of things we may be unconscious of. We are no different from employers, in that we also have our own fears. These fears may unconsciously cause us to sabotage our own job-hunt without even knowing it.

Following are some deliciously inventive ways to botch up an interview, with an explanation afterward of your mistake. Plus, what you should have done.

Example 1: It's OK for Me to Be Late . . .

Employer: OK, one of the things that this job requires is coming to work on time. We work together as a team here and all of us need to start the job at the same time. Is there anything that might get in the way of your coming in at 9 A.M. every morning?

Applicant: Well, as a matter of fact there is. I have epilepsy and can't drive, so I have to take the bus, and the bus is often late.

Your mistake: That the employer won't mind a change in standards because you are disabled. And that there is nothing you can do about the fact that the bus is late (i.e., take an earlier bus and get there early, so if you miss the first one, the next one will still get you there on time. Or find a car pool.)

What should have happened: Your research should have revealed that this employer had a rigid starting time. And you should have figured out how you were going to get there--or you should have been **determined** to find out. If you have disability-related reasons that make it extremely difficult to get to work at a specific time, find a job that has the flexibility you need. Today, flextime has become somewhat popular, and there are jobs that will make allowances.

Example 2: I Can't Deal with Stress . . .

Employer: This job has a lot of stress because you will have two and maybe three bosses. You are supervised by Don and Emma and they are not always great at coordinating assignments. And I supervise them--and although I try to always talk to them first, sometimes I don't and my own work takes priority. Now, have you ever dealt with multiple bosses and a lot of different projects at the same time?

Applicant: Well, that would be a disaster for me! I definitely can't deal with stress at all because of my disability. The three of you will have to have a meeting every morning and figure out my assignments and then maybe you could give them to me in writing.

Your mistake: This is what we call the "unreasonable accommodation" error. Your mistake is in thinking that you can tell the employer what to do and have them completely restructure the job and change their way of doing things because you have a disability.

What should have happened: There are two possibilities here. We are assuming that you would in fact have a challenge in dealing with this. If you still want the job, say something like, "Well, that sounds like college, where I had a lot of professors who certainly didn't coordinate their assignments. I simply managed my time so that everything could get done."

If you really don't want to work there after hearing their description, consider an explanation like this, "I really appreciate your frankness in telling me about the confusion I would be facing, and it might not be the best match for me. But, I am still an excellent worker -- very exacting and a perfectionist. In my last job, I was commended twice and given a cash award for my diligence. Do you know of a place that would appreciate those qualities enough that they would arrange for me to receive clear assignments from only one person?"

The employer just might refer you to another person -- and if you are really lucky and have mentioned a strength that they want, they *may* continue the interview and offer you the job -- and later figure out some way to make it easier for you.

Example 3: Oh, No -- I Can't . . .

Employer: If you accept this receptionist job, you will have to be able to use the computer and do some word processing.

Applicant: Oh, no. The only thing I can do is answer the phone, take messages, and greet people.

Your mistake: That you can make the job whatever you want rather than what the employer needs.

What should have happened: You should not be applying for a job as a receptionist. Almost all receptionist jobs require some word processing. You should have done informational interviews and studied various jobs to find one that would use your strengths and passion at greeting people and making them feel at home, say a hostess at a restaurant, flight attendant, even sales -- all jobs, by the way, that pay a lot more than a receptionist (and only rarely require extensive word processing).

Well, you get the picture. If you are failing to sell yourself to employers, you must figure out what you are doing wrong. **You must figure out how to sell yourself**.

ASKING EMPLOYERS FOR FEEDBACK

Unhappily, employers will hardly ever help you out here. You will *never* hear them say, "You did not do well in this interview because . . ."--and then spell it out (e.g., "You were too cocky and arrogant during the interview.") You will most likely be left completely in the dark about why you aren't getting hired. *Of course that's true of job-hunters without disabilities too. Employers rarely give* anyone *any feedback*.

One way around this deadly silence is through a mock interview. Some nonprofit groups and some career counselors offer this service. In it, you practice an interview, and then the counselor critiques it. Sometimes, the interview is videotaped, giving you the opportunity to see in living color what you actually did during the discussion. Then you can correct yourself, and practice more. If videotaping isn't offered as a service, ask a friend or someone in your family who has hired people to listen to some of your answers to interview questions and let you know how they would have felt if you were in their office trying to be hired.

You could also *ask* the people who interviewed you for helpful feedback. This sometimes works, *so long as* you make the inquiry *really general*. For example, after you've gotten turned down at a place, you might say, "You know, I've been on thirteen interviews now where I've gotten turned down. Is there something about me, besides my disability, that in your view is causing me not to get hired? If so, I'd really appreciate your giving me some pointers."

Most of the time, you *still* won't get a frank answer. You'll just get blithering generalities or else a killing silence. This is because of the employers' fear of lawsuits and such--and because **the world in general suffers for a lack of those**

who love us enough to tell us the truth. It's not just how they deal with you; it's how they deal with everybody.

But occasionally you will run into a loving soul, an employer who is willing to risk telling you the truth. No matter how painful it is to hear it, thank them from the bottom of your heart. Their advice, seriously heeded, can bring about just the changes in your interviewing strategies that you most need. Thank them, bless them.

OVERCOMING INTERNALIZED OPPRESSION

What kinds of fears make us sabotage our own job-hunt? What is the voice of disability oppression trying to tell us?

For starters, a few of us have fallen into the bad habit of *using* our disability to get what we want at home: time, attention, and love, based on the age-old principle of "the louder you sniffle, the more you get." We often get a great deal of sympathy for our helplessness, and we fear that going to work will mean the end of this whole way of life -- which we aren't sure we *want* to give up. We are afraid that maybe at work, people will treat us just like any other person. *Well, what can we tell you? You have to learn to overcome that fear.*

Another fear: Sometimes we have learned, through the long process of qualifying for disability benefits, that any information we volunteer (and particularly any positive information about our abilities) can and will be used against us. Hence, in the job interview, we are afraid to say very much about ourselves. Thus, we come across as trying to hide something. And under those conditions, we don't convince the employers of our qualifications. *Well, what can we tell you? You have to learn to overcome that fear.*

Next: If we've never held a job before, we often know very little about the nature of the world of work, how it performs, and what it's like. And we often have a minimum number of friends who could tell us. Since we don't know how to act, we

are afraid to go out in such an uncharted world. *Well, what can we tell you? You have to learn to overcome that fear.*

Sometimes we are afraid that if we get a job, we won't be able to "cut it." *Well, what can we tell you? You have to learn to overcome that fear.*

And then sometimes we are afraid to face our limitations, as putting ourselves to the test at a job would force us to do. *Well, what can we tell you? You have to learn to overcome that fear.*

We know, we know. All of that is easy to say. But how exactly *do* you overcome your fears? Practicing helps. So, for example, if you are concerned about knowing the proper things to do, ask people if you can "shadow" them on the job. Ask if you can simply follow them around and observe them for a half day or a full day. Many people will refuse but some will allow it. If they do, this gives you an easy way to watch social and work behaviors.

Simply make yourself **take the steps** that will get you a job. Call for one informational interview. Or simply start doing the Internet and library research--and when you are ready, call someone to ask questions. That is, those questions that might lead you to information about a person who has the power to hire you. . . .

This is called **courage**. Courage is not lack of fear. It is acting despite fear. And, unfortunately, it is required for most job-hunters in this country and particularly those people with disabilities who have the fears listed above.

There are ways to work directly on your own motivation. You can use "affirmations" where you tell yourself many times each day a positive statement that capsulizes the way you want to act. You might ask yourself questions that will bring out your motivation and cause you to act against your internalized oppression.

Read inspirational books by great authors and listen to motivational tapes. Consider taking some classes or joining a group of job seekers or attending a support group for people with your disability. Ask who is job-hunting and compare notes.

Find friends who will encourage you and hang around them. During your job-hunt, avoid people who are critical, negative, and demeaning. This, of course, does not mean surrounding yourself with people who only say what you want to hear. You want your network to include some constructively honest people who will be frank with you when you need it.

Also, don't overlook the possibility of seeking help from your spiritual life and from prayer (read "How to Find Your Mission in Life" in the 2002 version of *What Color Is Your Parachute?*). That has helped some job-hunters *immeasurably* in overcoming their fears. They learn that every experience becomes an adventure for two: God's spirit and you. Together, you can overcome all fear.

Eight Reasons for Hope

THAT ARE IMPORTANT TO THOSE OF US
WITH DISABILITIES
(AS WELL AS TO OUR WOULD-BE EMPLOYERS,
COUNSELORS, FRIENDS, AND FAMILIES)

**1. Everyone is disabled.
And everyone is employable.**

Let us suppose the human race had a Skills Bank, in which there were a total of 13,000 skills, and each one of us at birth had to go to that bank and choose 700 skills that we would use for the rest of our life here on earth. You and I, of course, would not choose the same 700. *You* might choose to be good at *analyzing things*, while *I* might choose to be good at *drawing*. And so forth. The varying skills we chose would make us different from one another, even unique.

But how would you describe yourself afterward? Would you point to the 700 things you can do, and do well? If so, you would be emphasizing **your abilities**. Or would you point to the 12,300 things that you still can't do--even if some *other* members of the human race can? If so, you would be emphasizing your **DIS**-abilities.

The point of this little fantasy is *everyone* has abilities, or things we *can* do. And *everyone* has **DIS**-abilities, or things we *can't* do. *(The numbers 700 and 13,000 were only chosen for the sake of illustration. No one knows how many skills the* *human race actually has, or how many a typical individual has.)* But, the numbers are unimportant. The *principle* is what is important.

In summary, everyone is **enabled**, and everyone is also **disabled.**

Everyone is **CAPable,** and everyone is also handi**CAP**ped. That's the nature of the life that is given to us all.

If you speak of yourself only as free, capable, and as a person with abilities, you are denying *the other side* of your nature. Or if you speak of yourself only as handicapped, disabled, and as a person with disabilities, you are denying the first side of your nature. Each and every human being is both sides.

In interpreting yourself to an employer, therefore, it is crucial for you to know this and emphasize this during an interview. You can put it quite simply: *"It's true I have a disability; all of us do. Every one of us has things we cannot do or cannot do well. But I am here because there are many things I can do and can do well. This is what they are . . ."* It is these abilities of yours that make you *eminently employable.*

Of course, to be able to say what they are, you *must* have done your homework on yourself. Some excellent ways of doing this homework are in *What Color Is Your Parachute?*, which this book supplements. You might also use the *What Color Is Your Parachute? Workbook.* The two books tell you how to determine exactly what it is you have to offer to the world. This involves identifying your gifts or talents, which is to say, your favorite skills, in order of priority or importance to you. In other words, you must *know what it is* that you can do well.

If you want the employer to think of you as both enabled and disabled--just like every other human being--you must be able to think of yourself that way too, even if you don't think of yourself that way all the time or have to fight the dark thoughts of internalized oppression. No matter what feelings come up, you must be able to *spell out your skills* in detail. And express the enabled part of your nature. Therein lies your hope.

> **2. Everyone is a member of many "tribes." And as a general rule, employers like to hire those whom they perceive to be members of their own "tribe."**

Since disability is a characteristic of us all, it follows that your disability ought never to stand in the way of your finding employment. Unfortunately -- as we all know too well -- it sometimes does, and those of us who happen to have visible disabilities need to know why.

The "why" seems obvious. We run into an obstacle, which is normally called "prejudice" or "discrimination." Trouble is, while this description is true, as far as it goes, it doesn't go anywhere near far enough. Thus, it ends up being a woefully inadequate description of our enemy. And when you don't know your enemy, it is almost impossible to win.

The truest description of the enemy we face in the job-hunt (and elsewhere) is **tribalism**. So, understanding tribalism is crucial to the success of your job-hunt. We are not speaking of "tribes" as understood by Native Americans; we are speaking in a more universal sense.

A "tribe" is any group that gives individuals a feeling of "**we**" as opposed to all *the others* out there who are "**them**." From way back in our history, we have always tended to organize ourselves into tribes, both in our thinking and in actuality.

"Them," the others, may be variously defined as those who belong to a different race, a different religious group, a different nationality, a different social status, or a different economic status, than we do.

Each of us usually belongs to *several* tribes. Our commitment to one tribe may be merely that of sympathy for others who are "like us" in this way or that, while our commitment to another tribe may be one of fierce loyalty and action unto the death, as in a clan or in a terrorist group. Tribes come in all sizes and shapes. They may be as local as a neighborhood, or as worldwide as a religion. They may be as small as a group of "buddies," or as large as a nation, flaunting fierce patriotism. We see them in clubs, we see them at sporting events, we see them at rallies, we see them at conventions, we see them in political parties, we see them in issues like abortion, we see them when families gather at holidays, and we see them in drug gangs.

While tribes *can* perform truly nobly -- they will sometimes give their own members sacrificial devotion and kindness -- on the whole, tribalism has created the darkest pages of humankind's history. Ethics that normally govern daily conduct are tossed out the window when dealing with other tribes. *One tribe is often singled out for particular contempt, disdain, epithets, hatred, and even physical violence.* Consider what we see in the Middle East, Bosnia, the former Soviet Union, China, and some African countries, to say nothing of our own country, with its racism, ageism, sexism, prejudice, and discrimination.

Even when tribes are rather benign in their conduct, they are rarely accused of showing any *sensitivity* to the needs and feelings of those who are not members of that tribe.

Tribalism not only devastates human relationships, it also alters the landscape. In any particular geographic area, we see the dominant tribe shaping the landscape and the environment to its own liking and its own needs, without much consideration for the other tribes who may be living off the same land. This insensitive domination could be seen as "handicapping" the other tribe or tribes. The dominant *tribe,* in this case *"the nondisabled,"* thinks of or calls the other tribe *the handicapped.*

In our country, of course, the dominant tribe in charge of human relations, the landscape, and the environment, is made up of people who have no real impairment of any "major life activity" -- in other words, *people without disabilities.* This tribe treats *the others* with great insensitivity, disdain, fear, and sometimes contempt and animosity. Naturally, this tribe has designed its roads, its transportation vehicles, its buildings, its doorways, its stairways, its amusement centers, its workplaces, its computer network, and its bathrooms to suit itself. It has also developed customs and communication patterns that suit itself. Needless to say, those who do not belong to this tribe, those who do have some impairment of "a major life activity," those with physical disabilities, mental illness, learning disabilities, or mental retardation, "the others," "them," often find it difficult to get around and work in that inimical environment.

Tribes, in addition to undermining human relations and altering the landscape, usually create their own distinctive language. And so it is that the dominant tribe in this country, referred to above, has a language that describes themselves as "we," "people with abilities," "normal" or "the able-bodied," while they call all the other tribes who *have* some impairment of "a major life activity" names such as "the others," "them," "people with disabilities," "the disabled," or "the handicapped." It would, of course, be accurate if they called us "those whom we have handicapped by the way we have shaped our environment and culture."

Here endeth our brief course on tribalism. Now, what does this all have to do with our job-hunt? Simply this: When those of us who happen to have disabilities go out job-hunting, we are unconsciously perceived as one tribe trying to find employment from another tribe. And the more *visible our disability* is -- that is, the *more* we are perceived as looking *different* from the dominant tribe (people without disabilities) -- the more *some* **employers will feel the force of this. And since as a general rule employers like to hire those whom they perceive to be members of their own tribe,** this is not good news. But it can be turned into good news, if you put your thinking cap on. Used rightly, tribalism can become the key to getting hired.

As we said earlier, everyone is a member of **many** tribes. Therefore, the key to your having a successful job interview is to ignore tribes as defined by ability or disability, and **find instead some other tribe** in which both you and your would-be employer are members. This is even more critical if you are also a person with a disability from a different ethnic background than the person you hope will hire you.

Did you both grow up in the same town? Then you are a member of *that* same tribe. Did you both go to the same school? Then you are members of *that* same tribe. Do you both have the same hobbies? Then you are members of *that* same tribe. Have you both traveled to the same places? Then you are members of *that* same tribe. Or do you both share a similar interest? Then you are members of *that* same tribe.

It is remarkable how many people know instinctively how important it is to establish this kinship in the same tribe. That is one reason it is good to **ask your tribe members to help you look for a job**. You belong to a church? Talk to the minister and congregation members. Are you part of a service club? Many of them will help you. Or, what about your college alumni association? They often publish newsletters with information about the jobs of fellow alumni. If you meet an employer **from your own tribe**, it will make it significantly easier to forge a connection.

Recently a job seeker approached one of the authors (Dale Brown) and said, "I hear you consider yourself to be an artist and are working on putting together exhibits of pictures and words." Dale began to enthusiastically explain about an exhibit she was working on, and the job seeker talked about her paintings. They discussed this common ground for several minutes before getting down to the actual meat of the discussion.

Making connections will be easier if you do enough research on that employer *before you go in* so you have discovered some commonality between you. Ask your contacts about them. Do a search for their name on the Internet. Read their home page if they have one. If you can't discover any such linkage *before* the interview, then *that discovery* must be your goal *during* the interview. Once that employer feels you are both members of the *same* tribe--despite your disability--you will have secured that most important of all qualities in a job interview: **rapport between you and the employer.** And this rapport is **the key** to your getting hired. Because, as we said, employers like to hire those whom they perceive to be somehow members of their own tribe.

---

3. People with disabilities are forming their own tribe or tribe (s).

People with disabilities are taking pride in their disabilities and identifying more and more as a person with a disability or a psychiatric system survivor, a Deaf person, a person who had polio, etc. About half (52 percent) of people with disabilities feel a "very" or "somewhat" strong sense of identity with other people with disabilities. This has increased from two out of five (40 percent) in 1986.[1] Grassroots groups took the lead in the passage of the Americans with Disabilities Act and the Ticket to Work and Work Incentives Improvement Act of 1999.

In 1988 students at Gallaudet University took a stand--they wanted a Deaf president. They shut down the campus and demanded that a Deaf president represent them, after the board of directors of the school appointed a hearing president. After marches, demonstrations, and a lot of lobbying in Congress, I. King Jordan, who was Deaf, was selected as president.[2]

Self-help groups of various sorts have flourished--giving people with varying disabilities, diseases, and conditions a

---

1. *1998 N.O.D./Harris Survey of Americans with Disabilities,* 30.
2. In a phone conversation with Dale Brown on February 15, 1999, Antonio Eades of the Public Relations Department, Gallaudet University.

chance to meet, share ways of coping, and take on projects that can make this country better for people with disabilities, such as persuading businesses to become accessible, filing complaints when they don't, persuading public libraries to buy low reading-level materials for adults, and the like.

These opportunities to meet other people with similar disabilities or to work in cross-disability coalitions can help your job-hunt in many ways. Discussions with people from your tribe will help you determine if problem X is because of discrimination or because of something that you could do better. You can get suggestions unique to your situation. Together, you can solve practical problems. And, the sense of community may help your self-esteem and cushion the "rejection shock" that is common to job-hunting. Some people with disabilities have actually organized "job clubs" among their disability group. All of the people meet on a weekly basis and keep each other on track.

Unfortunately, sometimes members of your tribe can make the job-hunt harder. For example, the feeling of *us the disabled* and *them* or *the others* can make it difficult to build rapport with the TAB (temporarily able-bodied) or AB (with each letter said aloud, standing for "able-bodied").

Some disability groups emphasize that they are *victims*. And *nobody* hires victims. The *anger* against a world that seems to exclude us may be quite justified. But it is hard to persuade the person with the power to hire you that you are one special employee out of two hundred, if you are angry with them. Your anger will come through.

Nevertheless, people with disabilities, on the whole, have a good record of helping each other be the best they can be. As a community or tribe we have passed laws, improved access, and taken charge of some government agencies that serve us. And we can also help each other find employment.

> ## 4. People with disabilities are getting better educated.

We know many of you are part of this trend. Good thing! Because employers are requiring more and more education and credentials. And lack of requisite skills and training were cited by two out of five employers as a possible barrier to the hiring and advancement of people with disabilities.[3]

In 1978, slightly less than three out of one hundred college freshmen were students with disabilities. Two decades later, in 1998, the percentage went up to nine out of one hundred.[4] This is partially because people with disabilities individually decided they wanted to get an education.

Another reason: Schools of higher education have become more willing to accept and educate students with disabilities. Schools are now more likely to be accessible to you. Most campuses have disabled student service centers where you can arrange for the specific assistance that you need. And professors are likely to have had at least one disabled student before you.

Unfortunately, this is not true of all schools. There are still prejudices and challenges. It requires effort and determination to get the best education possible. If you want more information on what higher education has to offer, contact HEATH Resource Center, the federal clearinghouse on higher education. Their phone number is 800-544-3284. More contact information is in the resource guide in Appendix C on page 141.

The Individuals with Disabilities Education Act (IDEA)

---

3. *The ADA at Work,* 5.
4. *The 1999 College Freshmen with Disabilities: A Biennial Statistical Profile,* prepared by the American Council on Education (Washington, DC: HEATH Resource Center/American Council on Education, 1999), 3.

requires youngsters with disabilities to receive a public education usually alongside their nondisabled fellow students. The law has been improved steadily since its inception in 1975, and more and more students have been "mainstreamed"--educated in ordinary classes--rather than "special education" classes. This means a better education--and a generation of young business leaders who have sat next to students with disabilities in their classrooms. They see them as fellow students and potential friends. And this may make them more open-minded when they face you across an interviewing desk.

---

5. Employers never hire a stranger.

Almost every job-hunter who happens to have a disability wants to find some magical way of avoiding meeting face to face with employers. (So do most job-hunters who *don't* have a disability, incidentally.) Of course we know that job-hunters *have* to meet face to face. But we hope that maybe we can plead that our disability is a reason to be let off the hook on this one. Especially if our disability is one of limited mobility. Perhaps *we* will be allowed to just communicate with the would-be employer by letter, e-mail, or by telephone.

No such luck! You may do some *preliminary* explorations by letter, e-mail, or by telephone, if you wish, but in the end you will *have* to go face to face. And risk rejection. Just like every other job-hunter. You, too, in a series of job interviews or in efforts to persuade the person with the power to hire you, will most likely hear the unnerving refrain--NO-NO-NO-NO-NO-NO-NO-NO-NO-NO-NO-NO-NO-NO-NO-NO-NO-NO-YES. This refrain is heard by those of us who happen to have disabilities, just as much as it is by those of us who don't happen to have disabilities (yet).

The reason why you *have* to go face to face with a would-be employer, in spite of the possibility of rejection, is that *employers never hire a stranger*. Nathan Azrin, a professor and the founder of the Job Club, was the first to emphasize this (see Appendix C, the list of written resources at the end of this book). What it means is that in order to decide to hire you, employers have to:

a. see you,
b. like you,
c. be convinced that there is something you can do for them, and
d. then feel that because of that, they've *got* to have you.

Notice the importance of "c" and "d" above. *Some* of us with disabilities think it only takes "a" and "b." *"Did you get the job?"* "Yes I did." *"Why did you get hired?"* "Because she liked me." Or, *"Did you get turned down for the job?"* "Yes, I did." *"Why did you get turned down?"* "Because he didn't like me."

Actually, the employer may have liked you a great deal. But if you couldn't tell them what you could do for them, then *that* is why you got turned down. Few, if any, employers are ever going to take the time to do this homework for you. That is not their responsibility.

It's important to recall just what a job *is*. In the beginning, someone decides to go into business for themselves. They want to sell a product, or information, or a service to others. To make this business succeed, they initially do *everything* themselves: making the product, or offering the service, or gathering the information all by their lonesome. In time, the business prospers, and it gets to be too much for one person to do. Our hero or heroine needs help.

What kind of help? Well, first of all they need someone to come and offer them **their time**. But they don't just need time. They need someone who, in that time, can **do the things they need to have done**. Maybe they have no time or skills to keep the accounting books. So they need someone who knows how to do accounting, and has the time to do it, to come and help them. In exchange for that time and those accounting skills, our hero or heroine is willing to give something in return: **money**. In other words, some of their profits. This exchange turns them into an employer, and the other person into their employee. And so, a job is born.

Now who are they going to hire? Well, usually, they hire someone they know. They try their friends. And ask everyone in their network. The one thing they will **not** do is to hire somebody they do not know. So, as we said earlier, you must go visit them. Or, if their office isn't accessible, and you won't have to work there, invite them to lunch -- or even to have a cup of coffee.

And you must help them to know you, *at least a little*, in the interview so they will be willing to offer you a job. How can you help them to know you? By telling them who you are: that is, what your abilities or skills are, and thus, what you have to offer them that would persuade them to part with some of their money.

This, unfortunately, is where the voices that oppress people with a disability as well as the rejection shock most job-hunters experience as they look for a job can get in the way. For if you go into *any* encounter with an employer with your attention focused on your disability, that is to say, if you focus on *who you are not*, rather than who you are, if you focus on what you *can't* do rather than what you *can* do, then there will be *no job offered* at the end of the encounter. Unfortunately, *even* if you focus on what you can do and who you are, there may *still* be no job if you let the employer get you off track with questions about your disability and *their* fears and concerns associated with it. This is especially true if they remain convinced of their misinformation about things you can't do. You **must** address their fears and stereotypes as we discussed earlier. If you do not, no job.

A bit of advice: Go home, and before you visit any other employer, sit down and figure out what you do well. If you can't figure this out by yourself, for one reason or another, get a mate, a friend, a counselor, to help you. Then learn to *talk about these strengths and learn to tell stories that demonstrate these strengths to the person who has the power to hire you.*

---

6. **The nation is changing its attitude toward people with disabilities in a positive direction-- from paternalism to productivity**.

There are two ways of looking at people with disabilities-- from a viewpoint of "**paternalism**" or "**productivity.**"

Under the **paternalism** viewpoint, people with disabilities are *to be pitied*, are objects of charity. The "good" employer has discharged their obligations by not letting you interview, because, you see, the job is too dangerous, too stressful, too difficult for a poor, pathetic person with a disability. Besides, people with disabilities have benefits-- they don't *have* to work.

Under the **productivity** viewpoint, *the above attitude is absolutely unfair.* People with disabilities say they want to be viewed as individuals-- to compete for jobs on a level playing field. They say they can contribute to the country if they are given a choice and a chance.

Many employers say they recognize the productivity viewpoint and realize that people with disabilities can be good employees. These employers are determined to be fair in their hiring and accommodation processes.

It has become more obvious to employers how wrong it is

to expect a class of people to remove themselves from the labor force. And how costly it is--some estimates say it costs up to $60 billion in benefits to keep people out of work versus $3 billion to help them get back to work. When the labor market is tight, employers need all the workers they can get. And that makes employers more open-minded toward the folks they tend to overlook--including people with disabilities.

According to a study of over eight hundred companies, approximately four out of five of them made accommodations to their employees including making facilities accessible (82 percent), changing the questions they asked during interviews (80 percent), and making interview locations (79 percent) and restrooms (78 percent) accessible to people with disabilities.[5]

True, there are some employers who won't hire you--they will pat you on the head, push you away, and not hire you no matter how good a job you do presenting yourself. But, we hope this book has shown you how to avoid this group and find the group who will look at your abilities objectively and consider hiring you. And there **are** more employers in that group than ever before.

> ## 7. In many places, ramps have replaced steps and access has improved.

You can see this all over the country--hopefully where you live. Buildings that used to have only steps--and maybe a freight elevator in the back--now have a ramp in front. More and more sidewalks have curb cuts, enabling someone in a wheelchair to easily get to the street--and a person with

---

5. *The ADA at Work,* 5.

knee problems to walk down more easily. Parking places designed for people with disabilities are frequently located near building entrances. Once all of these things were rare. Fifty-seven percent of people with disabilities, their families, and friends say that the ADA has resulted in better access to buildings.[6]

This not only helped people with disabilities, but people who are elderly and people with broken bones or other temporary situations. Universal design is a new philosophy that says that buildings, furniture, equipment, and other items that we use should be designed for all people--not just those people who are strong and can walk.

Accessibility makes a huge difference as we search for employment. You will run into some places where you cannot even apply because the only way to get to their offices is to go up steps. Or you might find a person willing to give you an informational interview, but getting to their office requires a special pass key from security before you can use the freight elevator. To get there, you have an exciting "roll" through a muddy back alley, plus someone to accompany you when you leave the freight elevator (which smells bad and is damp, cold, and dirty). Of course you want to clean up afterward-- but, guess what, the bathrooms are inaccessible too.

This still happens. But, it happens less and less. And the improvement in access is a reason for hope.

By the way, if such a scenario ever happens to you, remember that you are educating the organization that gave you all of the trouble. Not that educating people **should** be part of your job-hunt. But, believe me, after going through a lot of trouble to get you in the building, it is very likely someone will be very motivated to do something to make the building more accessible.

---

6. United Cerebral Palsy Associations, *1996 ADA Snapshot on America* (Washington, DC: United Cerebral Palsy Associations, 1996), 2.

And **this** scenario has happened more than once. A person with a disability followed the steps of creative job-hunting. They got a job offer. And their employer cheerfully made a bathroom accessible, built a ramp, and generally made it possible to get around. This is because the employer had been persuaded that they were hiring a person who is one in two hundred -- and they **really** needed this person on the job. So, they had to make sure the person could actually get to work.

The point we are making is that accessibility is improving. This shows the commitment of this country to include people with disabilities. It will help you find work.

---

8. **Everyone redesigns or modifies their job so as to highlight their abilities and get around their limitations.**

It is common for those of us who have disabilities to think that when we go job-hunting, we are going to have to request something unheard of in the world of work, namely, that the job be redesigned to accommodate our special limitations. *Wrong.*

Then, of course, a lot of us know that "reasonable accommodation" (the legal term for these modifications) is our **civil right** and get ready to demand that the employer make these changes to our job. *Also wrong.*

As Sidney Fine, a well-known expert on the labor market, has emphasized, *everyone* redesigns or modifies their job -- in minor ways or major. The reason for this is no job or no work environment exactly fits anyone, when they are first hired. The new job is like an ill-fitting suit. Inevitably, it *has* to be taken in, a tuck here, a tuck there; or it has to be let out, where it is pinching or hugging too tight -- before the person is able to do their best in that job. All of us have to alter, adjust, amend, revise, fine-tune, adapt, or shape each new job, in minor ways or major.

For example, let us say that a nondisabled person gets a job on an assembly line, where he is supposed to continually pick up a carton from a large stack of them that stands to his right. But he is left-handed. So, he redesigns his work space, and moves the stack of cartons over to the left side, in order that he may pick them up more handily. *He has redesigned or modified his job so as to highlight his abilities, and get around his limitations -- but no one thinks anything of it.*

Or, let us say a nondisabled person starts a job in an office, but is always cold. She might bring in a heater -- or even ask the employer to supply a heater. *She has changed her environment to make herself more productive and eliminate a barrier -- but no one thinks anything of it.*

Or, again, let us say a nondisabled person is an executive. Her predecessor always called her subordinates into her office, and listened to their summary of what they needed her decisions on. But *this* executive is more of *an eye person* than *an ear person.* She doesn't absorb their verbal summaries very well, when she is only able to hear them. So she redesigns their encounters, and asks them, in addition to their oral reports to her, to give her a one-page written summary of what they want her decisions on, and to wait until she has had a chance to read them. *She has redesigned or modified her job so as to highlight her communication abilities and get around her communication limitations -- but nobody thinks anything of it.*

Of course if you are the employee making this request of an employer, it is a little more difficult . . . and your diplomacy and persuasive abilities will be necessary. On the other hand, good managers *naturally and instinctively communicate with you the way you understand their requests.* They notice you didn't "listen," meaning you didn't do what they said. So, they write you a note to follow up next time. Then they notice you always do what they want when they write it down. So they keep on writing you notes and e-mailing you. So the manager, as part of the ordinary management process, *has redesigned or modified your job to highlight your abilities, and get around your limitations--but nobody thinks anything of it.*

Not just employees but employers also have gotten into this business of redesigning jobs--to get around the limitations of their employees. And often new technology has to be brought into play. For example, when employers realized that many of the employees they would have to hire couldn't add or subtract, they redesigned cash registers to tell the employee what change to give back to the customer, once they had keyed in the amount handed over by the customer. When employers in fast-food places realized that many of the employees they would have to hire couldn't read, they redesigned cash registers with pictures of the food, instead of words. When employers realized many of the employees they would have to hire couldn't remember instructions, they designed cash registers with screens on them that displayed the proper instructions, such as "close drawer."

And so we see that redesigning jobs, in order to accommodate the limitations of the person holding down that job, goes on *all of the time* in the world of work. It goes on without anyone even batting an eye, or thinking about it--until, of course, *we who happen to have some kind of obvious disability* walk in, asking for a job there. Then, when it becomes obvious that the price of hiring us is that the job will have to be partially redesigned or modified so as to highlight our abilities and get around our limitations--perhaps with some new technology, as above--the employer often acts as though we were asking for something no other job-hunter or employee has ever asked for.

The best thing to do is to tell the employer the truth. Tell them gently. Tell them nicely. But *tell* them: *"Employers and employees* continually redesign or modify jobs, so as to high-light employees' abilities and get around their limitations." Same goes for you; *no big deal.*

You might also tell them some stories about how modifications for people with disabilities improved the productivity of the entire operation -- especially if the story involves your disability and your career. For example, a man with one arm worked cutting microfiche. The engineering department built a "special" cutting machine for him. During his absence, everyone wanted to use it. It was easier for the people with two arms too. A visually impaired employee at a grocery store had trouble seeing the cash register. So the employer built one with bigger letters. Well, every time he was gone, the other employees *fought* to use his cash register.

You will be way ahead of the competition if, in addition to this general assurance, you can indicate more particularly **which tasks** you and the employer will need to redesign. *This will be relatively easy if* before you approach the employer for an interview, you first conduct conversations elsewhere with workers who actually do the work you would like to do.

That is why informational interviewing is so important.

If you haven't done it yet, you can do it by approaching potential fellow workers or people in other companies who do other jobs and say, "I need to come in and talk to somebody with your expertise, who can help me figure out if this job will work for me." Your goal is to find out what tasks make up that job *and* what skills it takes to do those tasks. Then you can isolate the **problem tasks** (for you). These will be the areas where you need to figure out some job redesign. You can then brainstorm ideas, or ask your friends to brainstorm ideas, or ask your career counselor to brainstorm ideas -- before you ever talk to the people who have the power to hire you for the particular kind of job that you are interested in.

And don't forget if you are really stuck, call 800-526-7234, the number of the Job Accommodation Network. Remember, they have trained counselors with a database of more than 250,000 past successful accommodations. They'll be glad to help you. (See page 52.)

If you *aren't* able to do this background research ahead of time, you might say to the employer, "Could you please give me an idea of how you have designed this job in your organization, and what tasks it requires to be done?" Then you may break the job down into those tasks you are perfectly able to do, and those tasks you and they would need to re-design.

OK, there you have it: a long explanation of eight strong grounds of hope for you in your job-hunt. If you feel more hopeful, now that these are clear in your mind, that empowers you. And you **do** want to feel powerful, strong, encouraged, and self-actualized when you go about the job-hunt. For, the basic principle of all job-hunting is: **If you want something to happen, it is you who must make it happen--with God's help**. That's as true for those of us with disabilities as it is for the nondisabled job-hunter.

APPENDIX A

Handling Special Situations

Each of you who is reading this book is unique. Each of you will be facing specific challenges. Three common circumstances are covered here: needing a counselor, getting off the benefit rolls and leaving Social Security so that you can work, and being new to the disability community.

GETTING HELP:
SHOULD YOU HIRE A COUNSELOR?

Sometimes, overcoming fear is so hard that you *really* need help. In these cases, consider a counselor. But you may not need one, and the job-search process we recommend does not require one. But you should seriously consider getting a counselor if:

- You have read this book several times, tried to start your job-hunt on numerous occasions, keep claiming that you will look for a job, but for some reason haven't gotten started yet. It seems mysteriously difficult to actually connect your finger to the buttons on the telephone and call someone. . . .

- You have been job-hunting with no success for six months or more. Or, you have been only spending a few hours a week at your job-hunt and can't seem to figure out what else to do.

• You just plain want help.

OK, you are ready to look for a counselor. Do you need a counselor who has been trained in helping people with disabilities (often called a rehabilitation or "rehab" counselor)? Or would a career counselor who works with the general population be better?

First, we need to say, whichever kind of counselor you choose, be extremely careful. Information about choosing a career counselor that does not specialize in disability can be found in an appendix of *What Color Is Your Parachute?* For most people, a regular career counselor is better, as they usually have a better grasp of the job market than those who specialize in disability. However, you will have to educate such a counselor about your disability. You will need to take the lead in doing the research on job accommodation and employment discrimination issues.

You would choose a counselor with specific training in working with people who have disabilities if:

• you have a particular need that must be addressed, such as lengthy time off for medical care, complicated accommodations, a big "gap" in your employment record, or a history of losing jobs;

• you have issues involving benefits such as Social Security and Medicare;

• you prefer someone with expertise in your disability.

Remember, however, just because someone is a rehabilitation counselor does not mean they know about your **particular** disability. So find out what the counselor does know.

The marks of **poor** (or burned-out) rehab counselors are: they have lost the ability to listen; they tend therefore to stereotype you rather than focusing on your uniqueness (you can just hear them thinking "I've heard this one before"); they only pay lip service to the idea that you can be independent, because in their heart of hearts they really believe the disabled need to be taken care of; they know the anatomy of disabilities, but not the anatomy of abilities; they give you their advice **before** they've heard you out; their basic need is to take care of people, and they set this personal need of theirs ahead of your best interests.

The marks of a **good** rehab counselor are: they have excellent rapport with their clients; they have high expectations of their clients; they feel it is in their client's best interest that the client should make the decisions concerning their life; their clients accomplish a great deal. They familiarize themselves with your file, if you have seen other counselors previously--but they do not accept other people's judgments about you, unless or until they see that behavior for themselves. They listen to what you tell them, make sure they understand, and the advice they give is based on what you said, combined with their experience and resources. If they have a personality conflict with you, they refer you immediately to someone who is more helpful. Furthermore, they research thoroughly what the disability is, rather than accepting clichés about it. Their basic role is to **act as a facilitator** for you, and their major contribution to your job-hunt is that they are skilled at helping you to identify your abilities and then identify a job that asks for just those abilities, so that when it comes time for you to fill out an application form at some company or organization, and you come to the question, "Do you have any disability that would keep you from performing *this* job?", you can truthfully answer, "No."

Before choosing **any** career counselor, interview at least three of them. Compare their programs on the basis of cost, their experience, and their success rate. Of course, you will avoid programs that promise you a job, that make you sign a contract as a condition of working with them, or demand money from you before they do any work.

You may want to talk to the counselor about your disability and the particular issues that concern you. Then, see if the counselor listens and responds intelligently. If you are considering hiring this person, provide some written information about your disability and ask them to read it.

If you have a counselor already, but after reading our description of good and bad counselors, you feel you've unwittingly fallen into the wrong hands, see if you can "redeem them." For example, if they keep limiting what you can do with statements such as "Don't do that, you'll lose this benefit or that," ask them for *written facts* that you can take home and study. Then assess the situation yourself and share what you find with them. If they tell you it is impossible to do such-and-such a job, call JAN yourself at 800-526-7234 -- and tell the counselor what you learned.

If it is not possible to redeem them, make your exit firmly and finally, and seek another counselor.

How do you find a counselor that specializes in people who have disabilities? Well, one free source of help available to you is Vocational Rehabilitation (often called "voc rehab"). It is a government-funded program that can help you get ready for work and find a job. In order to use it, you must be unemployed. If you already have a job, you are not eligible.

One great service offered by voc rehab is diagnosis of your disability and evaluation of your job skills. They need this information to determine if you are eligible for their services. Some people go to voc rehab strictly to get the evaluation. Additionally, they can offer job-seeking skills classes, help in looking for work, technological accommodations, help in paying for your education, classes in social skills, and sometimes job coaches. In some cases, they can pay for assistive technology. Unfortunately, you are not **entitled** to their help. You must apply and **they will decide if you are eligible**. In addition, many states have orders of selection and the most severely disabled people are served first. And sometimes, if your income is too high, you can't get certain services.

The best way to find the office nearest you is to contact:

National Rehabilitation Information Center
1010 Wayne Avenue, Suite 800
Silver Spring, MD 20910
Phone: 800-346-2742; 301-562-2400; 301-495-5626 (TTY)
Web site: www.naric.com

An information specialist will give you the phone number of your state rehabilitation agency, which will give you the address and phone number of your local office. By the way, if you are not well acquainted with the disability community or the services that are available to you, a trip to your voc rehab office might help you start networking, even if that one visit is all that you do. These offices are often central to what is going on to employ people with disabilities.

Vocational Rehabilitation is not the only source of rehabilitation counselors, however. Many nonprofit organizations provide counseling services. And there are rehabilitation counselors who work independently. Here are some national organizations that may help find a counselor living near you:

National Rehabilitation Association
633 South Washington Street, Suite 300
Alexandria, VA 22314
Phone: 703-836-0850; 703-836-0849 (TTY);
703-836-0848 (FAX)
Web site: www.nationalrehab.org

International Association of Rehabilitation Professionals
783 Rio Del Mar Boulevard, Suite 6
Aptos, CA 95003
Phone: 800-240-9059; 831-662-0310; 831-662-8487 (FAX)
Web site: www.rehabpro.org

National Rehabilitation Counseling Association

8807 Sudley Road, #102
Manassas, VA 20110-4719
Phone: 703-361-2077; 703-361-2489 (FAX)
Web site: nrca-net.org
E-mail: nrcaoffice@aol.com

RESOURCES FOR PEOPLE WHO ARE NEWLY DISABLED OR NEW TO THE DISABILITY COMMUNITY

If you are a person who was recently injured and are just now adjusting to life as a person with a disability . . . **or,** if you are a person who has always had a disability, but is just now choosing to enter the world of able-bodied people, as an independent person . . . **or,** even if you are a person with a disability who has just moved and needs to learn what is available in your area, here are some suggestions on how to find out what is available to you:

Talk to other people with disabilities. If you have one who is a friend, ask their advice. Ask everyone you know, "Do you know anyone who has a disability who seems to be active in the community and working?" You might even see someone in the street and go up to them and say, "I'm newly disabled; do you know anyone who can teach me the ropes?"

Call your local community college or university. Ask if they have a *Disabled Student Services Program.* They may be able to tell you what helpful services they have for you.

Visit or call one of the six hundred independent living centers in the United States, if there is one near you. The Independent Living Research Utilization Program would be happy to let you know of one that is in your area. They also publish a directory. Unfortunately, although you may be able to find an independent living center through networking, there is no standardized way to locate them in the phone book. Write or call:

Independent Living Research Utilization Program
2323 S. Shepherd, Suite 1000
Houston, TX 77019
Phone: 713-520-0232; 713-520-5136 (TTY);
713-520-5785 (FAX)
Web site: www.ilru.org

Visit or call the United Way. They usually maintain an information and referral directory, which includes services for people who have disabilities. To get connected to your local United Way, call 800-411-8929 (UWAY). They will ask you to enter your zip code and connect you.

Visit or call your local public library, particularly its librarian or reference librarian. Say to them, "I just became disabled. Could you help me find out who I can go to that could help me with counseling and the like?" If you are on your own in the library, look up "handicapped" or "disabled" in the vertical file and see what information you can locate for your local town or city. The U.S. Department of Justice routinely sends material on the ADA to public libraries.

Call your city or town government and ask if they have an information and referral service. See if they have a mayor's committee on employment of people with disabilities.

Also local *churches or synagogues* often will know about resources to help you, since frequently they have people with disabilities in their congregations.

Use the resources listed in Appendix B, in the section called "State and Local Resources for People with Disabilities."

RESOURCES AND INFORMATION FOR PEOPLE WHO ARE RECEIVING SOCIAL SECURITY BENEFITS AND ARE CONSIDERING GOING TO WORK

If you are receiving benefits from the government because you are disabled, and you have even gotten **the feeling in your heart and that gleam in your eye** that you want to work, we are very happy for you. Given the fact that you had to **prove** how disabled you are, **prove** that you were unable to work, and probably had to appeal an initial decision that denied you benefits--well, we are impressed that you are now seriously considering offering your talents to this great country--and we thank you.

For most people, the major problem with going back to work is a need to keep their health insurance. It is critical to assure that you will be able to keep your personal assistance service and the medical care you need to stay as independent, pain free, and energetic as possible.

Fortunately, as mentioned earlier in this book, the Social Security Administration is offering a number of incentives and services that lessen the risk. But, only you can decide whether or not you should work. So, these are the steps we recommend:

1. **Do a thorough assessment of your strengths, weaknesses, likes, dislikes, passions, and desires.** Take the extra time that being on benefits gives you to be extremely thorough and clear. If you want to offer yourself to employers, you need to know **what** you can offer. Do informational interviews--go out there and ask questions. Consider volunteer work, and get out in the community. These steps are often called "job readiness"--and they are critical to a successful start at work or return to work. For the most part, they will not put your benefits at risk, although you should check first. For example, if the government pays for your home-health services, they may stop payments if you are no longer "homebound."

2. **Research work incentives and disincentives.** You need to learn about the general principles behind the Americans with Disabilities Act, the Ticket to Work and Work Incentives Improvement Act of 1999, and the policies of Social Security. Figure out how going to work will impact your

particular situation. All of the information sources mentioned for the "newly disabled" in the earlier section will help you conduct this research.

To get general information, try:

- *The Social Security Administration's toll-free phone number:* 800-772-1213. They have an automated system with a menu of recordings. Hit "0" for a live person. If you are deaf, use the TTY number: 800-325-0778.
- *The Social Security Administration's Web site:* (www.ssa.gov/work) has many documents, some of which explain the work incentives very clearly. If you do not have personal access to the World Wide Web, try your public library, a cybercafé, or a school.
- *Your local Social Security office.* Each office has staff available to help the public, a rack of literature, and other information you can use.
- *Publications from the disability community* often discuss Social Security. Ask people in the support group involving your specific disability.

While doing your research, here are some "buzz-words," or specific work incentives you may want to ask about:

- *Impairment-Related Work Expense.* This benefit allows you to deduct the disability-related **costs of work** from the **pay you get** when determining your income for purposes of figuring out your Social Security benefit.
- *Medicare Buy-in or Continuation of Medicare.* If your state allows it, you can keep your valued health insurance after your benefits stop. Study this very carefully. For many disabilities, your health and independence require continued access to medical care. There is also a **Buy-in Program for Part A Medicare** (which covers hospitalization).
- *Plan for Achieving Self-Support (PASS).* If you are on SSI, you are only allowed a small amount of savings and assets. This makes it impossible to save for school tuition or tools

you might need to have on the job. PASS allows you to set aside money and/or things you own to reach your vocational goal. Your goal must be skills that pay well enough on the labor market to take you off SSI (not difficult -- SSI payments, as you know, are extremely low). The money you set aside for the PASS will not reduce your benefits. You can get a booklet on PASS from Social Security's toll-free number (800-772-1213). For specific information, you need to call your area's "PASS cadre." Those numbers are available on the Internet. Search the Social Security Web site: www.ssa.gov. Some local Social Security offices will be able to help.

- *Reinstatement of Benefits (expedited).* Previously, if you worked, and then lost the job, you had to reapply for Social Security, starting the long process over again. The law now provides a faster and less risky procedure. Find out details before you start your first day of work. Remember, it is possible to lose jobs through no fault of your own. On the other hand, once you work, you can save money and use your own resources as unemployment insurance.
- *Ticket to Work.* If you are in a state where the program has started, you can get a "ticket" that you can use to obtain services that will help you to work. To find out more, call 866-968-7842. They will explain whether you are in such a state and how to use your ticket. By January 2004, all states will be included.
- *Trial Work Period.* You can work for nine months, and the money in your paycheck will be added to your Social Security benefits. After your trial work period, you receive an **extended period of eligibility,** which means if your earnings fall below a certain amount, Social Security will give you some money to make up for it. An example of where this might help would be if your boss suddenly cuts your hours from full-time to part-time due to a business downturn.

3. **Figure out how the work incentives will affect your particular situation**. The problem you will face is that "the devil is in the details." Incentives will vary according to whether you have SSDI (Social Security Disability Insurance) or SSI (Supplemental Security Insurance). SSI is for people with low incomes. SSDI is for people who have worked, paid into the Social Security system, and are disabled and now need to collect benefits. Some people get both SSI and SSDI. Incentives will also vary according to which state you are in -- as most of the work incentives are left to the states to administer and set up the rules. Some states do a great job -- and others administer them so poorly, they are not useful to you.

Here are some ways to figure out how the details affect you specifically. First, gather all of your materials from the Social Security Administration that have come with your check or that you have received in the mail. List your income from benefits, other funds you get, and your expenses.

Second, go to your Social Security office and ask them if they have someone who specializes in people who want to go to work. These people might be called work incentive specialists. Or ask if there is an expert in PASS (Plan for Achieving Self-Support). You might also try asking who is responsible for liaison with Vocational Rehabilitation. If you find such a person, sit down with them and explain your situation.

If that does not work, then try some of the resources listed where we discussed people who are newly disabled or new to the disability community on page 120. You might also go directly to your local Vocational Rehabilitation office and ask to meet with a counselor. Explain that you are on Social Security and are interested in being rehabilitated so you can work.

4. **You may want to hire an attorney who specializes in Social Security law or a professional advocate or consultant.** There are some people who specialize in Social Security law. If you contact an attorney, they may be extremely surprised. Attorneys are used to people trying to get **on** Social Security -- not **off** Social Security. If you can't afford an attorney, try your local protection and advocacy agency or legal services. You can find a list on www.protectionandadvocacy.com. Try law schools and ask if they have legal clinics or a law student who might help you. Contact service clubs and ask if they have lawyers among their members, or if they would consider helping to pay for one. Be creative -- as a person with a disability who wants to work, you may find many allies. The fight to contribute is a battle that many may want to join. You might find people rallying to your side.

5. **Consider a "self-referral" for rehabilitation and employment services**. Do this if you are sure you want to go to work. Call 888-606-7787, the Social Security/Vocational Rehabilitation Service Hotline, and answer the questions you are asked. They will ask to access the information you provided Social Security. They will send you to Vocational Rehabilitation. If Vocational Rehabilitation does not serve you within four months, you will be referred to another nonprofit organization.

If you are not satisfied with the information obtained from the Social Security or other resources in this section, network in your state and local area. Keep saying to people, "I am on Social Security benefits, and I want to work. How can I do this without risking my health care and keeping a basic living income? I have heard that there are some changes in the law that might help me."

We realize it is possible that work is not right for you in your particular situation. We also realize that you have many fears. What we are asking -- **begging** might be a better word --is that you research the situation thoroughly. Don't assume Social Security laws are the same as they were in the past. The future regulations might be better than the present ones. Consider the possibility of working.

Take the time to sort out your strengths and weaknesses. Get out in the community and talk to people about how you can help. Even if you decide that in your case it is too risky and you don't go to work--you will have moved forward tremendously in your growth and development. And, if you do decide to work, you will find that your life and happiness will improve tremendously--and you will be making a valuable contribution to society.

Organizations and Resources to Help You

AND OTHER JOB SEEKERS WITH DISABILITIES

Basically, we are suggesting that you look for a job like anyone else would look. However, some programs are designed specifically for people with disabilities. They might be helpful, particularly if you don't know how to start your job-hunt, even after reading this book. Or if you are running into more than your share of discrimination. Or even if you simply want to use these disability-specific resources as part of your strategy. These programs will help you with job-search skills such as writing a resume, making a good impression during an interview, helping you find employers who are particularly open-minded to people with disabilities, or even providing jobs that will help you gain skills.

You must research these programs thoroughly before you get too involved. The good news is that most of these services are free. But, they may ask you to become a client of Vocational Rehabilitation or Social Security if you are not already. That is because they contract with these agencies who pay some of their operating costs.

Be a good consumer. The local components of each of these programs vary widely. When you ask for services, find out exactly what they offer. In your dealings with these organizations, ask yourself, does the staff treat you with respect? Do employers hire people who do the jobs that the organizations train you to do? Can they offer the names of graduates who will tell you about their experiences? If they say that for privacy reasons they can't give out that information, you might want to break out on your own and ask other people with disabilities. Some of these facilities hire people at less than the minimum wage if their productivity is low. Be sure that you honestly and clearly need a "practice job" before accepting less than minimum wage. Having said that, there are some rehabilitation facilities (once called "sheltered workshops") that have started people with disabilities in the work world who have gone on to reach their full potential. So in the following sections you'll find three unique national organizations that offer a variety of services.

NATIONAL ORGANIZATIONS

IAMCARES, a federally funded program with the International Association of Machinists, has local programs that help people with disabilities find employment. All of their jobs pay above minimum wage, and they offer help in connecting with a variety of jobs at many levels. Contact them at:

IAMAW Grand Lodge
  9000 Machinist's Place, Suite 101
  Upper Marlboro, MD 20772
  Phone: 301-967-4717
  Web site: www.iamaw.org/

Goodwill Industries is helpful to people who are not yet ready to work at a competitive job, but want a "practice job." Their jobs add tremendous value to the world, as they collect used goods and resell them, recycling valuable resources. They also may be able to refer you to helpful employers. Call 800-664-6577, press 1, then enter your zip code. This automatically connects you to your local Goodwill and gives you their number. Or contact them at:

Goodwill Industries
9200 Rockville Pike
Bethesda, MD 20814
Phone: 301-530-6500
Web site: www.goodwill.org

Easter Seals has affiliates in the majority of states in the United States. They operate placement offices that help people with disabilities find jobs, both through actual placement and by teaching job-seeking skills, such as interviewing and filling out applications. To find out if you have a local affiliate, call them at 800-221-6827. Or visit www.easter-seals.org, their Web site.

RESUME DATABASES

The National Business and Disability Council operates the NBDC National Resume Database for Persons with Disabilities, which enables qualified college graduates with disabilities to register their resumes. NBDC material states that Fortune 1000 companies, government agencies, and other organizations use their computerized databases. For a copy of the registration form, contact:

NBDC National Resume Database for People with Disabilities
c/o Future Tech Enterprises
101-7 Colin Drive
Holbrook, NY 11241
Phone: 800-839-6163; 516-465-1515
Web site: www.business-disability.com

Equal Opportunity Publications' Online Resume Database allows you to electronically send your resume to all advertisers in *Careers and the Disabled*. www.eop.com is the Web site.

These services are free and are probably worth a shot. Unfortunately, very few employers actually use resume databases. On one site, 85,000 job-hunters posted their resumes and only 850 employers looked at their resumes during a three-month period. Remember, most employers hire people they know and only go to resume databases as a last resort.

CONNECTING YOU TO INDIVIDUALS
WITH DISABILITIES

A number of programs will help connect you to people with disabilities who are working in areas similar to yours, even though it might not be the major goal of the program. For example, if you have a disability and a science background, the American Association for the Advancement of Science might be able to connect you with someone with a disability in a field similar to yours. Contact:

American Association for the Advancement of Science
Project on Science, Technology & Disability
1200 New York Avenue, NW
Washington, DC 20005-3920
Phone: 202-326-6400

If you are considering entering or restarting your career as an artist, VSA Arts, an international, nonprofit organization dedicated to encouraging artistic expression among people with disabilities, can help connect you with other artists with disabilities and offer you opportunities to exhibit. Contact:

VSA Arts
1300 Connecticut Avenue, NW, Suite 700
Washington, DC 20036
Phone: 800-933-8721; 202-737-0645 (TTY);
202-737-0725 (FAX)
Web site: www.vsarts.org
E-mail: creativespirit@vsarts.org

These are just two examples of organizations that will help. The way you find the ones that interest **you** is through research and networking.

RESOURCES FOR PEOPLE WHO ARE BLIND

The Job Opportunities for the Blind Targeted Job Initiative works only with people who are unemployed and eligible for Social Security. Potential clients also must be job-ready and able to work independently in an ordinary work environment. Staff are also willing to help any blind job seeker connect with other people who are blind and successful in their area. Contact:

Job Opportunities for the Blind
    National Federation of the Blind
    1800 Johnson Street
    Baltimore, MD 21230
    Phone: 410-659-9314; 410-685-5653 (FAX)
    Web site: www.nfb.org

Newsline for the Blind, administered by National Federation of the Blind, allows people who are blind or visually impaired to read some major national newspapers, including the classified job announcements, by telephone. Use the Web site above to find out more information and a listing of states in which the service is available.

America's Jobline The Telephone Job-Search Assistant allows people who cannot see print to use the telephone to review listings of job openings. The National Federation of the Blind, which administers it, and the Department of Labor, which funds it, are working toward having it in all fifty states and may have succeeded by the time you read this book. You use the key pad of a touch-tone phone to tell the system where you wish to work and what kind of job you want. You listen to each announcement, and can quickly move on to the next one if you decide you are not interested. You can store messages. You can set it up so you hear only the new announcements. Call 800-414-5748 to use the service.

STATE AND LOCAL RESOURCES FOR PEOPLE WITH DISABILITIES

One way to start networking in the disability services arena is to get a list of resources in your state. You can find various disability organizations in your telephone book and sometimes you can find one networker who can lead you to many of them.

Another possibility is to write or call the National Information Center for Children and Youth with Disabilities (NICHCY). Don't worry about the fact that they say they serve children and youth. They provide information for everyone--even though their major mission is children and youth. Ask for their list of resources for your state. That list will include:

- Your state Vocational Rehabilitation agency
- Your state coordinator of vocational education for students with disabilities
- Your state mental health agency
- Your state mental retardation program
- Your state developmental disabilities planning council
- The protection and advocacy agency (which will help you if you run into a situation that involves discrimination-- especially if you have a developmental disability)
- The client assistance program (where you can appeal a decision of Vocational Rehabilitation, for example, if they declare you not eligible for services)

Job-Hunting for the So-Called Handicapped

- Your regional center for technical assistance on the Americans with Disabilities Act
- A list of state chapters of organizations for particular disabilities such as autism, brain injury, cerebral palsy, epilepsy, spina bifida, and hearing loss

These organizations can lead you to the resources where you live.

The easiest way to get the list for your state is to visit their Web site at www.nichcy.org. If you don't have Web access, contact:

National Information Center for Children and Youth with Disabilities (NICHCY)
P.O. Box 1492
Washington, DC 20013-1492
Phone: 800-695-0285 (Voice/TTY);
202-884-8200 (Voice/TTY); 202-884-8441 (FAX)
E-mail: _NICHCY@aed.org

When networking with these state organizations, find the branch of the organization that is nearest to your city or town. Then look for local organizations that help people with disabilities find jobs. Following are a few that are particularly well known and established. They only refer you to jobs that pay minimum wage or above and are competitive, meaning that nondisabled people also apply for them. They list jobs within their own local area--but will work with someone who lives elsewhere and wants to move. If your city or area isn't listed below (and it probably isn't), network within the disability community. It is possible you will find a helpful agency.

Contact:
Project LINK
Mainstream, Inc.
6930 Carroll Avenue #240
Takoma Park, MD 20912

Phone: 301-891-8777 (Voice/TTY); 301-891-8778 (FAX)
Web site: www.mainstreaminc.org

Project LINK
Mainstream, Inc.
717 N. Harwood Drive, Suite 890
Dallas, TX 75201
Phone: 214-969-0118 (Voice/TTY)
214-969–0201 (FAX)

Just One Break, Inc.
120 Wall Street
New York, NY 10005
Phone: 212-785-7300; (212) 785-4515 (TTY);
(212) 785-4513 (FAX)
Web site: www.justonebreak.com
E-mail: jobs@justonebreak.com

OTHER SOURCES OF HELP

In 1999, the Office of Personnel Management set up a program to make **the federal government a model employer for people** with disabilities. A section of their Web site has been set up to offer materials on the program. It's address is:
http://www.opm.gov/disability.

For the most part, people with disabilities are encouraged to apply for federal jobs along with everybody else. However, many federal agencies have **selective placement coordinators** who can help you locate jobs at particular agencies. For a list, contact:

Office of Diversity
Office of Personnel Management
1900 E Street, NW
Washington, DC 20415-9800
Phone: 202-606-1059; 202-606-0927 (FAX)

Some federal agencies hire people with disabilities using trial appointments without competition. The manager may use this special appointing authority for a three-month period (up to seven hundred hours) before deciding if they want you permanently. This saves the manager a lot of paperwork. To use it, you must be certified by Vocational Rehabilitation as having a disability and being able to do the job.

If you can get certified, you could follow the steps of creative job-hunting. When it comes time to talk to the person with the power to hire you, tell them about this authority-- how they can hire you quickly without competition. If you've shown yourself to be the employee who can solve one or more of their major problems, they may take you up on it.

You may want to try your **One-Stop Career Center**. This is where almost every state has centralized its distribution of unemployment checks, employment services, and career-related training programs. Listings of jobs are usually available. Other services include counseling, job postings, assistance in filing unemployment insurance, and information on federal programs. Sometimes Vocational Rehabilitation is part of the one-stop center. To find your one-stop career center, call 877-872-5627, 877-889-5627 (TTY), or visit www.servicelocator.org.

Social Security offices were discussed earlier on page 121 and may be helpful sources of general information.

If you need information on **assistive technology** (gadgets, computer software, mechanical devices, or other technical products that can help you overcome your disability to do well on your job), contact your state Tech Act Project for Assistive Technology Services (called Tech Act projects). These centers offer help such as having equipment for you to try out or borrow, low-cost loan programs, funding for equipment, as well as friendly voices on the telephone that might steer you in the right direction.

To locate your state Tech Act project, contact:

RESNA Technical Assistance Project
1700 North Moore Street, Suite 1540
Arlington, VA 22209-1093
Phone: 703-524-6686
Web site: www.resna.org
E-mail: info@resna.org

INFORMATION ABOUT THE
AMERICANS WITH DISABILITIES ACT

Some government funded toll-free phone numbers may help you find specific information on the Americans with Disabilities Act.[1] Internet addresses are provided if you prefer to go online. Many of these numbers are underfunded and will lead you through call menus with lots of time on hold. It takes persistence and time to get a human being. Nevertheless, the people are usually helpful and they almost always provide accurate information. So the effort of calling them is worthwhile. Contact:

Disability & Business Technical Assistance Centers
Phone: 800-949-4232 (Voice/TTY)
Web site: www.adata.org

Disability Rights Education and Defense Fund (DREDF)
ADA Hotline
Phone: 800-466-4232 (Voice/TTY)
Web site: www.dredf.org

Department of Justice ADA Line for documents, questions, and referrals:
Phone: 800-514-0301; 800-514-0383 (TTY)
Web site: www.usdoj.gov

---

1. ADA Information Services, U.S. Department of Justice, Civil Rights Section, Disability Rights Division, Revised, February 2000.

The Equal Employment Opportunity Commission offers technical assistance on the employment provisions of ADA and how to file ADA complaints:
  Phone: 800-669-4000; 800-669-6820 (TTY)
  Web site: www.eeoc.gov

Department of Transportation offers technical assistance on the transportation requirements of the ADA:

ADA Assistance Line
  Phone: 888-446-4511; 202-366-2285;
  202-366-0153 (TTY)
  Web site: www.fta.dot.gov

The Access Board, also called Architectural and Transportation Barriers Compliance Board, offers information about access problems such as a building with no way in but a freight elevator -- or a bathroom you can't use. Included are access issues for other disabilities such as blindness and deafness. Documents and questions:
  Phone: 800-872-2253; 800-993-2822 (TTY)
  Web site: www.access-board.gov

IF ALL ELSE FAILS, CALL YOUR CONGRESSPERSON

Congressional offices usually have a "case manager" who can help you if you run into a dead end locally, if all of your calls to 800 numbers lead to "the zone of being on hold forever," and your letters are unanswered. You can say, "I'm a person with a disability, and I'm trying to find *this* kind of job, so I've located prospective employers and this is the problem I am running into. . . ." They may be effective working on federal government jobs or assuring that the government agencies do what they are supposed to do. They will be less effective with private-sector corporations. They may help you track down information that you need. Sometimes there's nothing they can do, but other times, they can be miracle workers.

It is good practice to write your congressperson from time to time about your positive and negative experiences with federal programs, such as Social Security, Vocational Rehabilitation, and the information centers you call through 800 numbers. You are a citizen--Congress oversees the federal agencies--and your letters make a difference. They may use what they read and hear to make improvements.

List of Written Resources

Books and magazines can assist your job search. They can help get you started -- or make you more knowledgeable as you go. As you network locally and nationally, get on as many mailing lists and subscribe to as many newsletters as you can. The habit of signing up for written material will give you lots of job leads, information about key events, and information about people that helps you to connect with them.

The same goes for the disability community (or tribe). You can learn the latest information on how to obtain help in looking for work as well as changes in the laws about benefits and who in the disability community is doing what. All of this may help you find the person with the power to hire you.

NATIONAL RESOURCE DIRECTORIES
FOR PEOPLE WITH DISABILITIES

Some people prefer to start networking for information about disabilities by getting an overview. They review all of the options before looking for what they want--and for those folks, there are two resource guides that may help:

HEATH National Resource Directory on Post-Secondary Education and Disability, available free, has organizations listed for specific disabilities, advocacy, architectural access, employment, independent living, recreation, funding, legal assistance, and other topics. HEATH is a national clearinghouse for information about post-secondary education for students with a disability, which means it can help you figure out how to get educated for the job you want. Contact:

HEATH Resource Center of the American Council on Education
One Dupont Circle, NW, Suite 800
Washington, DC 20036-1193
Phone: 800-544-3284 (Voice/TTY); 202-939-9320; 202-833-5696 (FAX)
Web site: www.HEATH-Resource-Center.org
E-mail: HEATH@ace.nche.edu or
gopher://bobcat-ace.nche.edu

Exceptional Parent Magazine sells an annual directory of national organizations, associations, products, and services at a reasonable price. Included are national organizations for specific disabilities, statewide listings of mental health resources, parent training and information centers, and more. Feel free to use parent resources even if you are an adult with a disability. They often have well-organized information, and will be glad to help you. To order a copy of the directory, contact:

Exceptional Parent
555 Kindermack Road
Oradell, NJ 07649

Phone: 877-372-7368; 201-634-6550; 201-634-6599 (FAX)
Web site: www.eparent.com

PERIODICALS TO CONNECT YOU WITH THE COMMUNITY OF PEOPLE WITH DISABILITIES

The following periodicals will allow you to learn about the challenges faced by other people who have disabilities. Employment issues are sometimes included.

Careers and the Disabled, Equal Opportunity Publications, Suite 200, 1160 Jericho Turnpike, Huntington, NY 11743 (516-421-9421). A quarterly magazine that has articles on looking for work, successful people with disabilities, and a "personal perspective" piece that describes the unique viewpoint of a job seeker, employer, or person with a disability. There are many recruiting advertisements. Mostly for recent college graduates or students who are starting their job search.

Ragged Edge, Box 145, Louisville, KY 40201. A journal with "attitude" that deals with all of the different feelings -- amid a wide range of vocabulary -- that are going on within people who happen to have disabilities. Nothing is off limits. Frank, and often graphic, especially in its language. Not for everyone, but has some very informative articles and debates in it.

New Mobility, P.O. Box 220, Horsham, PA 19044 (888-850-0344). A well-designed magazine that covers the issues of people who use wheelchairs for mobility. Includes all aspects of an active lifestyle: sexuality and relationships, job seeking and working, personal assistance care, sports, advocacy issues, and medical information such as the best type of wheelchair cushion.

Connections, P.O. Box 1269, E. Dennis, MA 02641 (617-739-2944, phone and FAX). Has articles and columns on all disabilities. Topics include legal issues, health matters, products, book reviews, and "local heroes."

We Magazine, 495 Broadway, 6th Floor, New York, NY 10012 (800-WE MAG 26). A slick lifestyle magazine for people with disabilities, mostly physical, but covers other disabilities. Includes sections on travel, eating out, current events specific to the disability community such as enforcement of ADA, and interviews with celebrities with disabilities.

ANNOTATED LIST OF BOOKS THAT PROVIDED BACKGROUND FOR *JOB-HUNTING FOR THE SO-CALLED HANDICAPPED*

These books and resources can help you with your job search. If there is something you are looking for, and you can't find it in your library, ask about an interlibrary loan and try a nearby university library. If that doesn't work, try the Library of Congress in Washington, DC.

Azrin, Nathan H. and Victoria A. Besalel. *Job Club Counselor's Manual: A Behavioral Approach to Vocational Counseling* (1980). Pro-Ed, 8700 Shoal Creek Blvd., Austin, TX 78757-6897 (800-897-3202; FAX 800-397-7633). Web site: www.proedinc.com. This is not a directory but a detailed description of a particular method of job-hunting called the "Job Club." Azrin invented the Job Club in 1970 in order to find a more structured way to help persons with disabilities as they went about their job-hunt. This manual explains in great detail how to set up such a club. In chapter 14 a section entitled "Evaluation of the Job Club with Job-Handicapped Persons" reports the success of this method with those who are disabled: 95 percent of those people with disabilities who were in the Job Club found jobs within six months compared to 28 percent in a non–Job Club control group. Don't forget, you do not have to be a counselor to organize a Job Club. If you are part of a support group of people with disabilities or have friends who are job seekers, you can work together in an organized manner. And you can use books by Richard Bolles as your texts.

Bolles, Richard Nelson. *What Color Is Your Parachute? A Practical Manual for Job-Hunters and Career-Changers* (revised annually, with each new edition appearing in November). Ten Speed Press, Box 7123, Berkeley, CA 94707 (800-841-2665 or 510-559-1600; FAX 510-559-1629). To order by e-mail, contact order@tenspeed.com. For more information, try the Web site: www.tenspeed.com. Available in almost all bookstores. This is **the** basic job-hunters manual. It should be "required reading" for all readers of this book, as this book is a supplement to it.

Bolles, Richard Nelson. *What Color Is Your Parachute? Workbook* (1998). Ten Speed Press. Contact information above. This workbook leads the job seeker or career changer step by step through the process of determining what sort of job or career they are most suited for and streamlines this most stressful and confusing process. Consider working with a group using this book as a text.

Bolles, Richard Nelson. *Job-Hunting on the Internet* (2001). Ten Speed Press. Contact information above. Describes what it is really like out there on the Internet--what you expect to be there versus what you actually find there. Lists large numbers of sites for job postings, resumes, career counseling, research sites, and contacts.

Brown, Dale S. *Learning a Living: A Guide to Planning Your Career and Finding a Job for People with Learning Disabilities, Attention Deficit Disorder, and Dyslexia* (2000). Woodbine House, 6510 Bells Mill Road, Bethesda, MD 20817 (800-843-7323; FAX 301-897-5838). Web site: www.woodbinehouse.com. E-mail: info@woodbinehouse.com. This book covers most aspects of the job-hunt in great detail. The sections on self-esteem and motivation will help most job-hunters. The book will interest anyone with a disability that cannot be seen--as there is a lot of information about disclosure and handling subtle discrimination.

SOME RECOMMENDED READING

These are books about jobs and careers written for the general public. We thought they might be helpful to you because they are particularly disability friendly.

Farr, J. Michael, *The Very Quick Job Search* (1996). JIST, 8902 Otis Avenue, Indianapolis, IN 46216-1033 (800-648-5478; FAX 317-613-4309). Web site: www.jist.com. E-mail: generaldelivery@jist.com. This book is recommended to those of you who are searching for your first full-time job after completing high school or college. Michael Farr has tremendous experience in the disability world, and his book has a curriculum that is often used in special education classes. He recommends creating JIST Cards, which are the size of an index card. Each has your contact information, your job objective, and skills written very briefly. He finds them harder to write, but far more effective than resumes. He also describes a JIST job interview as "any face-to-face contact with someone who hires or supervises people with your skills -- whether or not they have a job opening now." Individuals who follow his suggestions of going to two of these interviews a day are sure to find someone who will hire them -- as they will get to the employer before the competition does. Mr. Farr has published numerous other books, including *America's Top Resumes, The Quick Interview & Salary Negotiation Book,* and *How to Get a Job Now! Six Easy Steps to Getting a Better Job.* Write JIST for a catalog of their job-hunting materials.

Gaither, Richard. *The Wizard of Work: 88 Pages to Your Next Job* (1995). Ten Speed Press. Contact information on page 144. This book bills itself as a "simple, straightforward job-search book for people who'd rather be working than reading a book." It is short and sweet and has plenty of pointers. Included are disability issues such as how to dispel interview fears, whether or not to mention your disability, and the basics of the ADA.

Pimentel, Richard K., Christopher G. Bell, and Michael J. Lotito. *The Job Placement–ADA Connection* (1993). Milt Wright & Associates, 9548 Topanga Canyon Blvd., Chatsworth, CA 91311 (800-626-3939; FAX 818-349-0987; TTY 818-349-5031). Web site: www.miltwright.com. This book was written for placement and rehabilitation counselors--and it will help any job seeker who wants to learn their point of view. More importantly, there is a section, specifically for the job seeker, that goes into detail on handling the issue of your disability in a competitive interview. Legal details are provided.

SOME BOOKS AND BOOKLETS SPECIFICALLY FOR JOB SEEKERS WITH DISABILITIES

Epilepsy Foundation of America. *The Workbook: A Self-Study Guide for Job Seekers* (1991). Epilepsy Foundation of America, 4351 Garden City Drive, Landover, MD 20785-2267 (800-332-1000; FAX 301-577-9056). Web site: www. epilepsyfoundation.org. A sixty-four-page workbook for people with epilepsy that describes how to look for entry-level jobs using the numbers game. The book covers resumes, applications, using the telephone to uncover openings, interviews, and handling problems on the job once you have it. It includes an excellent table on disclosure of the disability, when you should disclose, and the advantages and disadvantages of each time within the process. It may be useful for anyone with a medical condition that limits them, but is not immediately visible.

Forster, Wayne. *Six Steps to Employment for People with Disabilities* (2000). Cambridge Educational 90 MacCorkle Avenue, SW, South Charleston, WV 25303 (800-468-4227; FAX 800-329-6687). A workbook aimed at setting career goals, assessing strengths, writing resumes, completing application forms, being interviewed, and handling follow-up. Uses the numbers game approach of searching for openings and applying for them. Forster uses the analogy of a businss selling a product.

Kendrick, Deborah. *Teachers Who Are Blind or Visually Impaired* (1998). AFB Press, American Foundation for the Blind, 11 Penn Plaza, Suite 300, New York, NY 10001 (800-232-3044; FAX 412-741-0609). Profiles eighteen teachers who are blind or visually impaired with an account of the details that constitute a day's work. Each profile includes the teacher's photograph, age, and visual acuity as well as the equipment they use, and vivid details of daily activities. It will be extremely helpful for any person with a visual impairment who is considering teaching as a career--and it should be read by any administrator who has doubts about whether blind teachers can do the job. Larger print and well laid out.

Roessler, Ph.D., Richard T., and Phillip Rumrill. Ph.D. *The Win-Win Approach to Reasonable Accommodations: Enhancing Productivity on Your Job* (1995). Education Department, National Multiple Sclerosis Society, 733 Third Avenue, New York, NY 10017-3288. To obtain a free copy, call 800-FIGHT-MS (800-344-4867) and press 1. This will connect you with your local chapter of the MS Society, which currently has the responsibility for distribution.

Although this material was written for people with multiple sclerosis, it will be helpful to you if you have an adult-onset medical condition that impacts your work. It gives a thorough discussion of reasonable accommodation, types of accommodations, how to make an effective request, and your legal rights.

Ryan, Daniel J. *Job Search Handbook for People with Disabilities* (2000). JIST Works, Inc. Contact information on page 145. A great basic job-search handbook that covers many of the issues that come up for people with disabilities. Aimed at people looking for their first job, it describes resumes, cover letters, networking, interviewing, getting the job offer, and keeping the job after you get it. Includes information about accommodation, the ADA, and discrimination. The book mostly describes the numbers game.

VSA Arts. *Putting Creativity to Work: Careers In the Arts for People with Disabilities* (2000). VSA Arts, 1300 Connecticut Avenue, NW, Suite 700, Washington, DC 20036. A detailed guide to making a living in the arts (including writing, acting, and visual arts). Financing an education and choosing a school are described. The book covers looking for arts-related employment and gives information on the specifics needed to sell each type of art. Benefits such as Social Security and Medicaid are covered thoroughly.

ANNOTATED LIST OF SELECTED REPORTS AND SURVEYS USED TO RESEARCH THIS BOOK

If you are interested in learning more about employment of people with disabilities, you might study these documents:

The ADA at Work: Implementation of the Employment Provisions of the Americans with Disabilities Act (1999). Society for Human Resource Management, Cornell University School of Industrial & Labor Relations, The Lewin Group, and Washington Business Group on Health, 39 pages. Available from the Society for Human Resource Management, Issues Management Program, 1800 Duke Street, Alexandria, VA 22314-3499 (703-548-3440). A report describing a survey of 1,402 members of the Society for Human Resource Management who were chosen to proportionately include small, medium, and large organizations. Tells how employers are reacting to the ADA. A few highlights: (1) Many organizations are making ADA-related accommodations. (2) Employers find making accommodations is easy. (3) Respondents are not as familiar with accommodations for people who are deaf or blind. (4) Lawyers are the most used resource for answering questions regarding the ADA.

The ICD Survey II: Employing Disabled Americans, International Center for the Disabled (March, 1987). Conducted by Lou Harris and Associates, Inc. Commissioned by the U.S. Department of Labor and the U.S. Department of Health and Human Services, Survey 864009, Louis Harris & Associates, 111 Fifth Avenue, New York, NY 10003. The second of two Harris Polls on managers' attitudes toward employees with disabilities. The first was done in 1986. It is a real disappointment to people studying these issues that there are no further surveys. We used this report judiciously, only in places where we felt the data was still relevant. Includes management assessment of people with disabilities, attitudes toward job discrimination, hiring policies, ratings of job performance, information on the cost of employment and accommodation, and rehabilitation of employees who become disabled. If anyone out there who funds research reads this, please consider doing a similar survey **now.** We are very curious to find out how the ADA and other trends have changed the attitudes of managers.

1998 N.O.D./Harris Survey of Americans with Disabilities. Conducted by Lou Harris and Associates, Inc. Commissioned by the National Organization on Disability, Survey 828373, Louis Harris & Associates, 111 Fifth Avenue, New York, NY 10003. This survey of 1,000 Americans with disabilities, aged sixteen or older, is conducted regularly. Information is included on employment, obstacles encountered at work, education, quality of life, leisure time activities, access to health care, and political involvement.

1999 College Freshmen with Disabilities: A Biennial Statistical Profile, Statistical Year, 1998. HEATH Resource Center and American Council on Education, 44 pages. Single copies available free from HEATH Resource Center, American Council on Education, One Dupont Circle, NW, Washington, DC 20036-1193 (800-544-3284, Voice/TTY). Summary of statistics relating to disability from a major national survey of college freshmen. Includes information on types of disability, percentage of students with disabilities, race, gender, political opinions, self-perceptions, life objectives, and reasons why they chose particular colleges.

Chartbook on Work and Disability in the United States, 1998. U.S. National Institute on Disability and Rehabilitation Research, an InfoUse Report, Washington, DC, 60 pages. Document is available on the Web site: www.ed.gov/ offices/OSERS/NIDDR/pubs.html. For more information, contact: U.S. Department of Education, OSERS/NIDRR, Switzer Building, Room 3431, Washington, DC 20202 (202-205-5633). Describes the state of work and disability in the United States through a series of charts from various surveys. Includes prevalence of disability among working-age people, work disability and the labor force, median earnings, health conditions, benefits received, and various breakdowns by age, gender, and race.

P.S. TO EMPLOYERS

Do use employees with disabilities to the fullest of their abilities. Don't put them in a repetitious, safe, dead-end job, just so that you won't have to spend any time on them. If you hire someone with a disability, be prepared especially to give them some time and attention during the training period. Since many employers are prone to take shortcuts in this area with **all** of their employees, hiring someone with a disability can have a salutary effect on your whole organization, as you have impressed upon it anew the importance of training for all.

If any of your employees with disabilities aren't meeting your standards, tell them so, early on. If problems arise with their performance, don't wait too long to intervene. There are problems that can be solved, if they are tackled early enough, and tackled jointly.

If the person you hire screws up on the job, don't blame it on their disability. Blame it, as you would any other employee, on human nature. If you have to let them go, again don't blame it on the disability or start gossip with other employers you know, along the lines of, "Well I hired a disabled person, but it just didn't work." One poor employee who has a disability doesn't say anything about other employees with disabilities. It's better to stop such gossip before it starts.

If a nondisabled person at your company becomes disabled, do go and visit them. A visit from you is important. Say, "We miss you, and we want you back." If you are in a position to offer some economic help toward getting them back on the job, do it. Your organization will realize cost savings by not having to recruit and train someone else. And you will get this experienced and devoted employee back on the job, even if in modified or alternative work. In addition, you will show your other employees that you will not desert them when the going gets rough.

Index

About the Authors

RICHARD N. BOLLES

Richard N. Bolles is acknowledged as "the most widely read and influential leader in the whole career planning field" (U.S. Law Placement Association) and as "the one responsible for the renaissance of the career counseling profession in the U.S. over the past decade" (*Money* magazine). He is the author of the most popular career-planning and job-hunting book in the world, *What Color Is Your Parachute? A Practical Manual for Job-Hunters and Career-Changers*, with over 6,000,000 copies in print. Revised and updated annually, it is purchased by over 20,000 people a month and exists in twelve languages. The book has been on the *New York Times* best-seller list 288 weeks thus far in its lifetime and was selected by the Library of Congress (Center for the Book) as one of twenty-five books that have shaped readers' lives (the list includes the Bible, *The Little Prince*, and others).

Mr. Bolles is author of a number of other books, including *Job-Hunting on the Internet*, and *The Three Boxes of Life, And How to Get Out of Them: An Introduction to Life/Work Planning*. He coauthored (with Howard Figler) *The Career Counselor's Handbook* and (with the late John Crystal) *Where Do I Go from Here with My Life?* He maintains a free Web site for job-hunters at www.JobHuntersBible.com, and travels extensively as a speaker or consultant.

The author's background is in engineering, physics, theology, and career counseling. He is an alumnus of the Massachusetts Institute of Technology in chemical engineering; Harvard University in physics (where he graduated cum laude); and the General Theological (Episcopal) Seminary in New York City, from which he holds a master's degree in

New Testament studies. Mr. Bolles's background includes service as canon pastor of Grace Cathedral, San Francisco, 1966–68; national staff member of United Ministries in Higher Education, 1968–87; director, National Career Development Project, 1974–87; and author, consultant, and speaker, since 1970.

DALE S. BROWN

Dale S. Brown is a nationally known expert and advocate for getting people with disabilities to work. She was a key player in the passage of the Americans with Disabilities Act. She is widely credited with founding the self-help movement for people with learning disabilities.

She is the author of *Learning a Living: A Guide to Planning Your Career and Finding a Job for People with Learning Disabilities, Attention Deficit Disorder, and Dyslexia* and *Steps to Independence for People with Learning Disabilities*. She wrote a commercially successful book of poetry titled *I Know I Can Climb the Mountain*. She coauthored (with Paul J. Gerber, Ph.D.) *Learning Disabilities and Employment*, a research compendium published by Pro-Ed. She has written hundreds of published articles on various aspects of employment and social skills. She writes *Dialogue with Dale*, a interactive Web site column with LD Online (www.ldonline.org).

She has spoken on topics related to disability and employment at more than one thousand international, national, state, and local conferences and symposia. She serves or has served on numerous national and local boards of directors, including the Council on Quality and Leadership in Supports for People with Disabilities, the ENDependence Center of Northern Virginia, and the Congressional Task Force on the Rights and Empowerment of Americans with Disabilities. Since 1988, she has led support groups for people with dyslexia at the International Dyslexia Association.

The awards for her work on improving the lives of people with disabilities include the Ten Outstanding Young Americans Award from the United States Junior Chamber of Commerce and the Arthur S. Flemming Award for Excellence in Civil Service Administration. She is listed in *Who's Who of the World*.